EMOTIONAL INTELLIGENCE

MASTERING MEANINGFUL CONNECTIONS AND SUCCESS

MD MEHEDI HASAN EMON

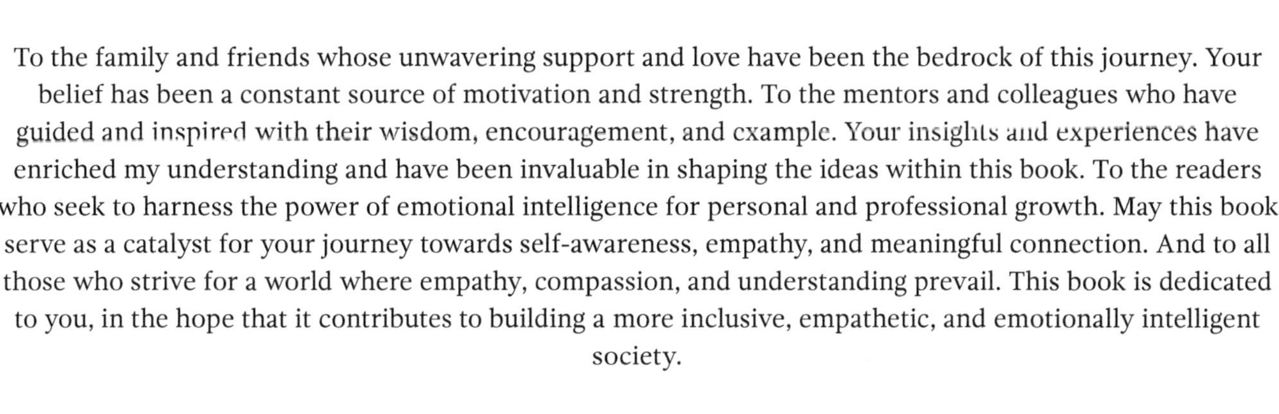

To the family and friends whose unwavering support and love have been the bedrock of this journey. Your belief has been a constant source of motivation and strength. To the mentors and colleagues who have guided and inspired with their wisdom, encouragement, and example. Your insights and experiences have enriched my understanding and have been invaluable in shaping the ideas within this book. To the readers who seek to harness the power of emotional intelligence for personal and professional growth. May this book serve as a catalyst for your journey towards self-awareness, empathy, and meaningful connection. And to all those who strive for a world where empathy, compassion, and understanding prevail. This book is dedicated to you, in the hope that it contributes to building a more inclusive, empathetic, and emotionally intelligent society.

Contents

Foreword

In a world where the pace of life seems to accelerate with each passing day, the importance of emotional intelligence cannot be overstated. As we navigate the complexities of personal and professional relationships, the ability to understand and manage our own emotions, as well as empathize with others, becomes crucial. Emotional Intelligence: Mastering Meaningful Connections and Success is a timely and invaluable guide that delves deep into the core of emotional intelligence, offering readers the tools and insights needed to thrive in an increasingly interconnected and dynamic world.

As someone who has witnessed firsthand the transformative power of emotional intelligence, I am delighted to introduce this comprehensive and insightful book. The authors, Md Mehedi Hasan Emon, Tahsina Khan, Dr. Md. Adnan Rahman, Dr. Zakari Bukari and Most. Sharmin Ara Chowdhury, bring a wealth of knowledge and experience to this work. Their diverse backgrounds and professional expertise converge to create a rich tapestry of practical advice, research-backed strategies, and real-life examples that will resonate with readers from all walks of life.

This book is structured to provide a clear and logical progression from understanding the foundational concepts of emotional intelligence to applying them in various aspects of life. The chapters cover a wide range of topics, including self-awareness, motivation, empathy, social skills, and leadership. Each chapter is meticulously crafted to ensure that readers not only grasp the theoretical underpinnings of emotional intelligence but also learn how to implement these principles in their daily lives.

One of the most compelling aspects of this book is its emphasis on practical application. The authors provide actionable steps and exercises that readers can incorporate into their routines, fostering continuous growth and improvement. Whether you are a student, a professional, a leader, or someone seeking personal development, this book offers valuable insights and practical guidance to help you harness the power of emotional intelligence.

Moreover, the book's focus on empathy and meaningful connections is particularly pertinent in today's world, where digital communication often overshadows face-to-face interactions. The authors eloquently highlight the importance of cultivating empathy and understanding, demonstrating how these qualities can lead to more fulfilling relationships and a more compassionate society.

As you embark on this journey through the pages of Emotional Intelligence: Mastering Meaningful Connections and Success, I encourage you to approach the content with an open mind and a willingness to embrace change. The concepts and techniques presented in this book have the potential to transform not only your personal and professional relationships but also your overall approach to life's challenges and opportunities.

In conclusion, this book is more than just a guide to emotional intelligence; it is a roadmap to a more empathetic, connected, and successful life. The authors' dedication to helping others achieve their full potential is evident in every chapter, making this book a must-read for anyone committed to personal and professional growth.

I am confident that Emotional Intelligence: Mastering Meaningful Connections and Success will inspire, inform, and empower you to become the best version of yourself. May your journey through this book be enlightening and transformative.

Sincerely,

Prof. Dr. Lydia Bennett

Preface

Welcome to the exploration of emotional intelligence – a journey that delves deep into the realm of human emotions, relationships, and personal growth. In today's fast-paced and interconnected world, the significance of emotional intelligence cannot be overstated. As we navigate the complexities of modern life, our ability to understand and manage our emotions, communicate effectively, and build meaningful relationships plays a crucial role in determining our success and well-being.

This book is designed as a guide for individuals seeking to enhance their emotional intelligence and unlock their full potential. Whether you're a student embarking on your academic journey, a professional striving for career advancement, or simply someone looking to enrich your personal relationships, the principles of emotional intelligence presented here offer valuable insights and practical strategies for growth.

In the pages that follow, we will explore various facets of emotional intelligence, from self-awareness and self-regulation to empathy, social skills, and leadership. Each chapter is dedicated to examining a specific aspect of emotional intelligence in depth, providing a comprehensive understanding of its importance and practical techniques for development.

Throughout this journey, we will draw upon real-life examples, scientific research, and time-tested wisdom to illuminate the path forward. By integrating theory with practical application, we aim to empower you to cultivate emotional intelligence in your own life and reap the rewards it offers – from improved relationships and enhanced well-being to greater success and fulfillment.

As you embark on this journey of self-discovery and growth, I encourage you to approach it with an open mind and a willingness to explore new perspectives. Embracing the principles of emotional intelligence requires dedication, patience, and practice, but the rewards are well worth the effort. Together, let us embark on this transformative journey towards greater self-awareness, empathy, and personal mastery.

Acknowledgements

First and foremost, we extend our deepest gratitude to Allah, the Most Gracious and Most Merciful. It is through His blessings and guidance that we have been able to undertake and complete this project. We thank Allah for giving us the strength, wisdom, and perseverance to bring this book to fruition.

To our colleagues at Manuscript Mastery Advisors Ltd., Bangladesh University of Professional, and Daffodil International University, we are immensely grateful for your support and encouragement throughout this journey. Your insights, feedback, and camaraderie have been invaluable in shaping the direction and content of this book. We are fortunate to work alongside such talented and dedicated individuals who continually inspire us to strive for excellence.

A special note of thanks to our students and mentees, who have been a source of inspiration and motivation. Your curiosity, dedication, and passion for learning have fueled our own enthusiasm for this subject. It is for you and future generations of learners that we have endeavored to create a resource that is both informative and transformative.

To our families, who have been our unwavering pillars of support, we owe our heartfelt appreciation. To our parents, who instilled in us the values of hard work, perseverance, and integrity, thank you for your endless love and guidance. To our spouses and children, who have patiently endured our long hours and absences, your understanding and encouragement have been our driving force. This book would not have been possible without your constant support and sacrifices.

We also wish to acknowledge the contributions of all those who have played a role in the creation of this book, whether through direct involvement or by providing moral support. Your belief in our vision and your encouragement have been instrumental in bringing this project to life.

Lastly, to our readers, thank you for your interest and trust in our work. We hope that Emotional Intelligence: Mastering Meaningful Connections and Success serves as a valuable guide on your journey towards personal and professional growth. It is our sincere hope that the insights and strategies shared in this book will help you cultivate deeper connections, foster empathy, and achieve lasting success.

With heartfelt thanks,

Md Mehedi Hasan Emon

Tahsina Khan

Dr. Md. Adnan Rahman

Dr. Zakari Bukari

Most. Sharmin Ara Chowdhury

Prologue

In a world that is increasingly interconnected and complex, the ability to navigate human emotions and relationships has become a crucial skill. The digital age, while enhancing our connectivity, has also posed challenges to the depth and authenticity of our interactions. Amidst this backdrop, emotional intelligence (EI) has emerged as a vital competency, enabling individuals to understand, manage, and effectively express their emotions, as well as navigate the emotions of others.

This book, Emotional Intelligence: Mastering Meaningful Connections and Success, is born out of a profound recognition of the transformative power of emotional intelligence. It seeks to provide a comprehensive exploration of EI, not just as a theoretical concept but as a practical tool that can be harnessed to enhance personal and professional life.

Our journey in writing this book began with a shared realization: that true success and fulfillment are not solely determined by intellectual capabilities or technical skills, but by our ability to connect with others, understand their perspectives, and manage our own emotional landscapes. We observed that individuals who excel in these areas tend to lead more fulfilling lives, achieve their goals more effectively, and build stronger, more meaningful relationships.

Throughout our careers, we have witnessed the profound impact that emotional intelligence can have on individuals and organizations. We have seen how leaders who practice empathy and self-awareness can inspire their teams, how educators who understand the emotional needs of their students can foster a more conducive learning environment, and how individuals who manage their emotions well can navigate life's challenges with resilience and grace.

In this book, we have distilled our experiences, insights, and research into a practical guide that aims to empower you to develop and enhance your own emotional intelligence. Each chapter delves into a different aspect of EI, providing not only theoretical understanding but also actionable strategies that you can apply in your daily life.

As you embark on this journey, we invite you to reflect on your own emotional experiences, to practice the skills discussed, and to embrace the growth that comes with greater emotional awareness and understanding. The path to mastering emotional intelligence is ongoing, requiring commitment and practice, but the rewards—deeper connections, greater empathy, and a more fulfilled life—are well worth the effort.

We are honored to share this journey with you and hope that this book will be a valuable companion in your pursuit of emotional intelligence and the meaningful connections and success that it can bring.

With warm regards,

Md Mehedi Hasan Emon

Tahsina Khan

Dr. Md. Adnan Rahman

Dr. Zakari Bukari

Most. Sharmin Ara Chowdhury

CHAPTER ONE

THE FOUNDATIONS OF EMOTIONAL INTELLIGENCE

1.1 Emotional Intelligence

Emotional Intelligence (EI) is the ability to understand and manage our own emotions, as well as recognize and influence the emotions of others. While traditional intelligence (IQ) measures cognitive abilities like logical reasoning, problem-solving, and analytical skills, EI focuses on the emotional and social aspects of human interaction. It involves a range of skills that help individuals navigate social complexities, build relationships, and make informed decisions based on emotional understanding.

The concept of EI was popularized by psychologist Daniel Goleman in the mid-1990s, although the idea was initially introduced by researchers Peter Salovey and John D. Mayer in 1990. Goleman identified five key components of EI: self-awareness, self-regulation, motivation, empathy, and social skills. These elements collectively help individuals understand their own emotions, manage them effectively, stay motivated, empathize with others, and navigate social situations skillfully.

To understand EI better, let's look at a practical example involving a student named Anika from Greenfield University.

Anika is a diligent and hardworking student who often feels overwhelmed and anxious before her exams. Despite her consistent efforts and good preparation, she finds herself unable to focus during exam periods, which affects her performance. Anika's anxiety stems from a deep-seated fear of disappointing her parents, who have high expectations of her academic success. Initially, Anika struggles to understand why she feels so anxious, often thinking that perhaps she isn't studying hard enough or isn't capable enough. However, she decides to start keeping a journal to document her feelings and experiences. This practice of journaling is a significant step towards developing self-awareness, one of the core components of EI. Through her journal entries, Anika begins to notice a pattern. Her anxiety peaks whenever she thinks about her parents' expectations and the possibility of not meeting them. This realization helps her understand that her fear of disappointing her parents is the primary source of her anxiety, not her lack of preparation or ability. Recognizing this is a crucial aspect of self-awareness. She now understands her emotions better and identifies the underlying cause of her stress. Armed with this new understanding, Anika decides to take further steps to manage her anxiety. She schedules an appointment with the university counselor to discuss her feelings and seek professional guidance. The counselor helps Anika develop strategies to cope with her anxiety, such as mindfulness exercises, relaxation techniques, and positive affirmations. These strategies help Anika regulate her emotions better, which is an important aspect of self-regulation, another component of EI.

Self-regulation involves managing one's emotional responses, particularly in stressful situations, to stay calm and composed. Anika learns to practice deep breathing and mindfulness meditation, which helps her stay focused and calm before her exams. By implementing these techniques, she notices a significant reduction in her anxiety levels, allowing her to perform better in her exams.

Additionally, Anika starts setting personal goals that are aligned with her own aspirations, rather than just meeting her parents' expectations. This shift in perspective helps her stay motivated and driven, another key aspect of EI. Intrinsic motivation, which is driven by personal satisfaction and a sense of achievement, helps individuals stay committed to their goals and overcome obstacles.

Anika also finds inspiration in a simple yet powerful quote: **"I changed myself for myself."** She tries to believe in herself with just this one quote, using it as a mantra to reinforce her self-worth and determination. This positive self-affirmation becomes a cornerstone of her motivation, helping her to stay focused on her personal growth and development. Furthermore, Anika begins to empathize with her parents' perspective. She understands that their high expectations stem from their desire for her to succeed and have a bright future. This empathy helps her communicate more openly with her parents about her feelings and stress. She explains her perspective and discusses her goals and aspirations with them. This open communication improves their relationship and reduces the pressure she feels, demonstrating the importance of empathy and social skills in EI. Social skills, which include effective communication, conflict resolution, and building positive relationships, play a crucial role in managing interpersonal dynamics. Anika's ability to articulate her feelings and understand her parents' perspective helps create a supportive environment where her emotional well-being is prioritized. Anika's journey illustrates how emotional intelligence can positively impact various aspects of life, from academic performance to personal relationships. By understanding and managing her emotions, Anika not only improves her exam performance but also builds stronger, more empathetic relationships with her parents. Her story highlights the importance of EI in navigating life's challenges and achieving personal and professional success.

1.2 The Five Pillars of Emotional Intelligence

Emotional Intelligence (EI) consists of five key components, often referred to as the five pillars. These pillars help us understand and manage our emotions and navigate social interactions more effectively. Let's explore each of these pillars and see how they manifest in everyday life.

1.2.1 Self-Awareness

Self-awareness is the ability to recognize and understand our own emotions. It's like having a mirror for our feelings, reflecting why we feel a certain way in different situations. This pillar of Emotional Intelligence (EI) allows us to monitor our emotions and thoughts, giving us insight into how they influence our behavior. Understanding our emotions is crucial because it helps us respond to situations more effectively. For instance, if you feel a sudden surge of anger during a meeting, self-awareness helps you identify the source of this anger, whether it's due to feeling unheard or from stress built up from previous events. By acknowledging and understanding these emotions, you can manage your responses better, rather than reacting impulsively.

Anika often feels nervous before giving presentations at work. This anxiety affects her performance, making her voice tremble and her mind go blank. To tackle this, Anika starts keeping a diary where she writes down her thoughts and feelings. Through her diary entries, she realizes that her nervousness stems from a fear of being judged by her colleagues. This newfound awareness helps Anika understand the root cause of her anxiety. With this understanding, she begins practicing her presentations in front of friends to build her confidence. Recognizing the source of her fear and addressing it directly helps Anika feel more prepared and less anxious during her presentations.

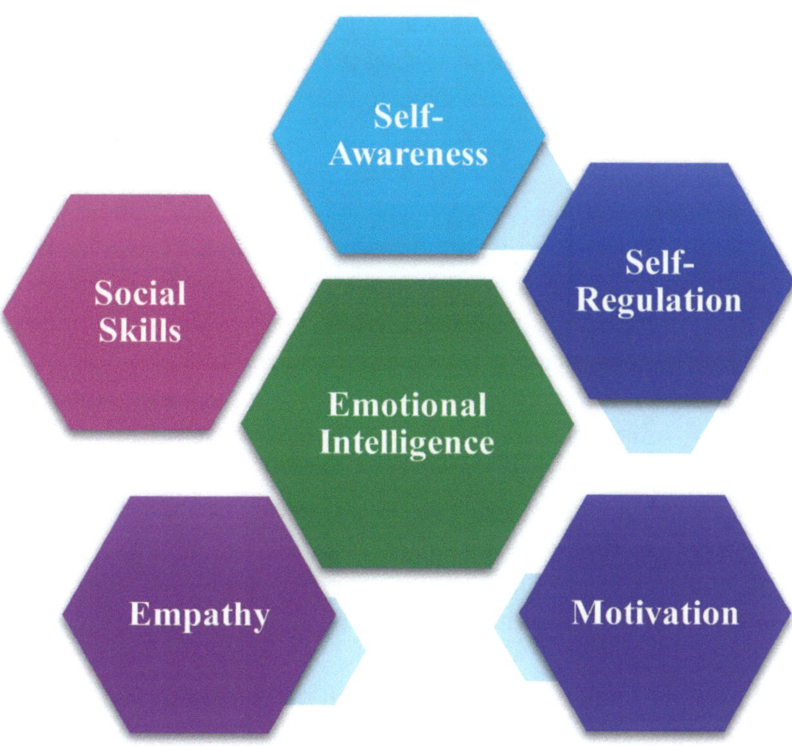

Five Pillars of Emotional Intelligence

1.2.2 Self-Regulation

Self-regulation involves managing our emotions, particularly in stressful situations, to remain calm and composed. It's about controlling impulses and reacting thoughtfully rather than impulsively. This skill is crucial for maintaining emotional stability and making rational decisions, even when under pressure. When we encounter stressful situations, our initial response is often driven by instinctive emotional reactions. For instance, if someone criticizes our work, our immediate impulse might be to react defensively or angrily. However, self-regulation helps us pause, assess the situation, and respond in a more measured and constructive way. It allows us to keep our emotions in check and prevent them from overwhelming our ability to think clearly.

Ahid often gets frustrated when his project team members don't meet deadlines. His initial reaction is to get angry and confront them, which creates tension within the team. However, after learning about self-regulation, Ahid decides to take a different approach. Instead of reacting with anger, he takes deep breaths to calm himself down and then schedules a team meeting. During the meeting, he calmly discusses the importance of deadlines and asks for suggestions on how the team can manage their time better. By regulating his emotional response, Ahid fosters a more collaborative and productive environment.

1.2.3 Motivation

Motivation in Emotional Intelligence (EI) refers to having a strong drive to achieve goals for personal satisfaction rather than external rewards. It involves staying committed and passionate about personal and professional goals, driven by an inner desire to succeed and improve rather than by external incentives like money, status, or approval from others. Intrinsic motivation is essential for long-term success and fulfillment. When we are intrinsically motivated, we find joy and satisfaction in the process of pursuing our goals, not just in the outcomes. This kind of motivation helps us stay focused and resilient, even when faced with challenges or setbacks. It fosters a sense of purpose and direction, encouraging us to keep moving forward regardless of obstacles.

Anika loves learning new things and sets small, manageable goals for herself, like reading one new article or learning a new concept every day. This intrinsic motivation keeps her engaged and excited about her personal development, even when facing challenges. Instead of feeling pressured by external validation, Anika finds joy and satisfaction in the learning process itself. Her internal drive to learn and improve helps her stay focused and achieve her goals.

1.2.4 Empathy

Empathy is the ability to understand and share the feelings of others. It's about putting ourselves in others' shoes and experiencing their emotions as if they were our own. This skill is crucial for building strong, meaningful relationships and for effective communication. Empathy allows us to connect with others on a deeper level. When we empathize with someone, we are not just acknowledging their feelings but are also validating their experiences. This validation can be incredibly powerful, making others feel heard and understood. It helps to create a supportive and trusting environment where people feel comfortable sharing their thoughts and emotions.

Ahid notices that his friend Alishba, who is usually very active and cheerful, has been unusually quiet and withdrawn. Concerned, he approaches her to ask if everything is alright. Alishba confides in him that she is going through some family problems, which is affecting her mood and performance at work. By listening to her without judgment and offering his support, Alishba shows empathy. He understands her emotional state and provides a comforting presence, helping Alishba feel less alone in her struggles. Ahid's empathetic response strengthens their friendship and shows how understanding others' emotions can positively impact relationships.

1.2.5 Social Skills

Social skills encompass the ability to effectively interact with others, build relationships, and manage conflicts. These skills are essential for forming connections and working collaboratively with others in various social and professional settings. Effective communication lies at the heart of social skills. It involves not only expressing oneself clearly but also listening actively and empathetically to others. Good communicators can convey their thoughts and ideas in a way that is easily understood and can also understand the perspectives and feelings of those they are communicating with. Building relationships is another key aspect of social skills. This involves establishing rapport, showing genuine interest in others, and nurturing connections over time. Strong relationships are built on trust, respect, and mutual understanding, and individuals with strong social skills excel at fostering these qualities in their interactions. Furthermore, social skills encompass the ability to navigate social dynamics and manage conflicts constructively. This involves resolving disagreements, negotiating compromises, and finding solutions that satisfy all parties involved. Individuals with strong social skills can defuse tense situations, build consensus, and maintain harmony in their interpersonal interactions.

Anika takes an active role in organizing community activities and social events. She notices that some people in her community feel isolated and disconnected. Anika uses her social skills to bring these people together, creating groups where they can support and learn from each other. She also organizes social events to help people connect on a personal level, fostering a sense of community and belonging. Her ability to interact effectively with a diverse group of people, mediate conflicts, and build strong relationships helps create a friendly and cooperative atmosphere in her community.

1.3 The Science Behind Emotional Intelligence

Emotional Intelligence (EI) is not just a concept; it's deeply rooted in the biology of our brains. Understanding the science behind EI helps us grasp how our brains process emotions and how developing EI can lead to various benefits in our lives.

1.3.1 The Brain and Emotional Intelligence

Different parts of our brain play crucial roles in emotional processing and regulation. The amygdala, often referred to as the brain's emotional center, is responsible for processing emotions, particularly fear and pleasure responses. When we encounter a situation that triggers an emotional response, such as feeling anxious before a presentation or happy when spending time with loved ones, the amygdala becomes activated. However, emotional intelligence involves more than just experiencing emotions; it also encompasses our ability to manage and regulate them effectively. This is where the prefrontal cortex comes into play. The prefrontal cortex, located in the frontal lobe of the brain, is responsible for higher-order cognitive functions, including decision-making, impulse control, and emotional regulation. It helps us evaluate situations, weigh options, and exert control over our emotional responses. When we encounter a stressful situation, such as receiving criticism from a colleague or facing a tight deadline, the prefrontal cortex helps us regulate our emotions and make rational decisions rather than reacting impulsively. It allows us to pause, assess the situation, and choose the most appropriate course of action based on our goals and values.

1.3.2 The Benefits of High Emotional Intelligence

Numerous studies have demonstrated the profound impact of emotional intelligence on various aspects of our lives. People with high EI tend to experience a range of benefits, including better physical and mental health, improved performance at work, and enhanced leadership skills.

Healthier Individuals: Research has shown that individuals with high EI are more likely to experience better physical health and overall well-being. They tend to have lower levels of stress, anxiety, and depression, as they are better equipped to manage their emotions and cope with life's challenges effectively. By regulating their emotions well, they can prevent stress-related illnesses and maintain a healthier lifestyle.

Improved Performance at Work: Emotional intelligence is highly valued in the workplace, as it contributes to better interpersonal relationships, effective communication, and conflict resolution skills. Employees with high EI are better able to collaborate with colleagues, adapt to change, and navigate complex social dynamics in the workplace. As a result, they often perform better, are more productive, and contribute positively to team success.

Enhanced Leadership Skills: Effective leadership requires more than just technical expertise; it also involves strong interpersonal skills and the ability to inspire and motivate others. Leaders with high EI excel in building trust, fostering a positive work environment, and providing support and guidance to their team members. They are empathetic, approachable, and able to connect with others on a deeper level, which enhances team cohesion and performance.

1.4 Assessing Your Emotional Intelligence

Assessing your Emotional Intelligence (EI) can provide valuable insights into your strengths and areas for improvement, helping you develop a deeper understanding of yourself and enhance your interpersonal skills. Several tools have been developed to measure EI, with the Emotional Quotient Inventory (EQ-i) and the Mayer-Salovey-Caruso Emotional Intelligence Test (MSCEIT) being among the most popular ones.

The Emotional Quotient Inventory (EQ-i)

The Emotional Quotient Inventory (EQ-i) is a self-report assessment designed to measure various aspects of emotional intelligence. It consists of several subscales that assess different components of EI, including self-awareness, self-regulation, empathy, social skills, and motivation. The EQ-i provides individuals with a comprehensive overview of their emotional strengths and weaknesses, allowing them to identify areas for personal and professional development. When taking the EQ-i, individuals respond to a series of questions or statements related to their emotions, thoughts, and behaviors. Their responses are then scored to generate a profile of their emotional intelligence. The results provide insight into how they perceive and manage their emotions, as well as how they interact with others in social and professional settings.

The Mayer-Salovey-Caruso Emotional Intelligence Test (MSCEIT)

The Mayer-Salovey-Caruso Emotional Intelligence Test (MSCEIT) is an ability-based assessment that measures emotional intelligence by evaluating individuals' cognitive abilities related to emotions. Unlike self-report assessments like the EQ-i, the MSCEIT presents participants with tasks and scenarios that require them to identify, understand, and manage emotions effectively. The MSCEIT assesses four branches of emotional intelligence: perceiving emotions, using emotions to facilitate thinking, understanding emotions, and managing emotions. Participants complete various tasks, such as identifying emotions in facial expressions, solving emotional problems, and predicting emotional outcomes in social situations. Their responses are then scored based on the accuracy of their emotional reasoning and problem-solving abilities.

Ahid's EI Assessment

Ahid, a student at Innovation University, decides to take an EI test as part of a course on personal development. He completes the EQ-i and discovers valuable insights into his emotional strengths and areas for improvement. According to the results, Ahid excels in understanding others' feelings and demonstrating empathy, indicating strong social awareness and interpersonal skills. However, the assessment also reveals that Ahid struggles with managing his own stress and regulating his emotions effectively in challenging situations. Armed with this knowledge, Ahid recognizes the importance of improving his self-regulation skills to enhance his overall emotional intelligence. He decides to focus on strategies for managing stress and coping with pressure more effectively. Ahid begins practicing mindfulness techniques, such as deep breathing and progressive muscle relaxation, to calm his mind and body during stressful moments. He also learns to identify his triggers and develop healthier coping mechanisms, such as taking breaks, seeking social support, and reframing negative thoughts. Over time, Ahid's efforts pay off, and he notices significant improvements in his ability to regulate his emotions and cope with stress more effectively. By leveraging the insights gained from his EI assessment, Ahid develops greater self-awareness and enhances his emotional intelligence, ultimately leading to personal growth and improved well-being.

1.5 The Role of EI in Personal and Professional Success

Emotional Intelligence (EI) plays a pivotal role in both personal and professional success. It encompasses the ability to recognize, understand, and manage emotions—both our own and those of others. Individuals with high EI are better equipped to navigate the complexities of human interactions, leading to more fulfilling relationships, effective leadership, and overall well-being.

Professional Success

In the workplace, EI is highly valued as it contributes to various aspects of professional success. People with high EI are often regarded as effective leaders and valuable team members due to their ability to communicate effectively, manage conflicts, and inspire others. Here's how EI influences professional success:

1. Leadership: Individuals with high EI make great leaders because they can motivate and understand their team members. They are empathetic, approachable, and able to connect with others on a deeper level. A leader with high EI can foster a positive work environment, build trust among team members, and inspire collaboration and innovation.

Example: Anika, a recent graduate from Aspire University, leverages her EI skills to secure a management position in a leading company. Her ability to empathize with her team members and stay calm under pressure earns her their respect and trust. Anika's leadership style focuses on fostering open communication, providing support, and recognizing the unique strengths of each team member. As a result, her team thrives under her guidance, achieving remarkable results and driving the company's success.

2. Teamwork: EI is essential for effective teamwork and collaboration in the workplace. Individuals with high EI are skilled at building rapport, resolving conflicts, and fostering a sense of camaraderie among team members. They can understand and appreciate diverse perspectives, communicate their ideas clearly, and adapt to different working styles.

3. Communication: Effective communication is a cornerstone of professional success, and EI plays a crucial role in enhancing interpersonal communication skills. Individuals with high EI are adept at expressing themselves clearly, listening actively, and understanding non-verbal cues. They can convey their thoughts and ideas in a way that resonates with others, leading to better teamwork, decision-making, and conflict resolution.

Personal Success

Beyond the workplace, EI also contributes to personal success by fostering healthier relationships, improving communication, and enhancing overall well-being. Here's how EI influences personal success:

1. Relationships: EI is key to forming and maintaining strong, meaningful relationships. It allows individuals to express their feelings clearly, understand others' emotions, and build supportive connections based on trust and empathy. People with high EI are better equipped to navigate relationship challenges, communicate effectively, and resolve conflicts constructively.

Ahid, studying at Summit University, utilizes his EI skills to navigate conflicts with his roommates and create a more harmonious living environment. By practicing empathy, active listening, and problem-solving, Ahid fosters open communication and mutual respect among his roommates. As a result, they are able to address issues constructively, compromise when necessary, and cultivate a supportive living space where everyone feels valued and understood.

2. Well-being: EI contributes to overall well-being by helping individuals manage stress, regulate their emotions, and cope with life's challenges effectively. People with high EI are more resilient in the face of adversity, as they can adapt to change, bounce back from setbacks, and maintain a positive outlook on life.

1.6 Common Misconceptions About Emotional Intelligence

Emotional Intelligence (EI) is a complex and multifaceted concept that is often misunderstood. Despite its growing recognition and importance in various aspects of life, there are several common misconceptions surrounding EI that warrant clarification. Let's explore some of these misconceptions and debunk them:

1. EI is Just About Being Nice

One of the most prevalent misconceptions about EI is that it simply involves being nice or pleasant to others. While empathy and kindness are indeed important components of EI, it goes beyond mere politeness. EI encompasses a wide range of emotional competencies, including self-awareness, self-regulation, empathy, social skills, and motivation.

Debunking the Misconception: EI involves not only understanding and managing our own emotions but also recognizing and responding to the emotions of others. This includes making tough decisions, providing constructive feedback, and effectively managing conflicts. Individuals with high EI can navigate challenging situations with tact and empathy, even when faced with difficult decisions or conflicts.

Imagine Anika, a team leader in a fast-paced work environment. Despite having to deliver critical feedback to a team member, Anika approaches the situation with empathy and professionalism. She acknowledges the individual's contributions while providing constructive criticism, ultimately fostering a supportive and growth-oriented work culture.

2. EI Cannot Be Learned

Another common misconception is that EI is an inherent trait that cannot be learned or developed. Some people believe that individuals are either born with high EI or not, and that it cannot be cultivated through practice or training.

Debunking the Misconception: Contrary to popular belief, EI is a skill that can be learned and improved with intentional effort and practice. Like any other skill, developing EI requires self-awareness, commitment, and continuous learning. Through self-reflection, feedback, and targeted interventions, individuals can enhance their emotional competencies and become more emotionally intelligent over time.

Consider Ahid, a medical student who initially believes that EI is not relevant to his field of study. However, after attending a workshop on EI in healthcare, Ahid realizes the importance of empathy and good communication in patient care and teamwork. Inspired by this realization, Ahid commits to developing his EI skills through role-playing exercises, communication workshops, and reflective practice. As a result, Ahid becomes more attuned to the emotional needs of his patients and colleagues, ultimately enhancing the quality of care and collaboration in his medical practice.

3. EI is Irrelevant in Professional Settings

Some individuals mistakenly believe that EI is only relevant in personal relationships and has little to no impact in professional settings. They may perceive emotions as a distraction or hindrance in the workplace, overlooking the significant role that EI plays in leadership, teamwork, and job performance.

Debunking the Misconception: EI is indeed crucial in professional settings, influencing various aspects of organizational effectiveness and individual success. Leaders with high EI are better equipped to inspire and motivate their teams, foster a positive work culture, and navigate complex interpersonal dynamics. Moreover, EI enhances communication, collaboration, and conflict resolution skills, leading to improved teamwork and job performance.

In a corporate setting, Anika, a manager with high EI, demonstrates effective leadership by building trust, fostering open communication, and promoting a culture of accountability. Her ability to understand and respond to the emotions of her team members enables her to address conflicts constructively, resolve issues, and facilitate collaboration. As a result, Anika's team achieves higher levels of productivity, engagement, and satisfaction, contributing to overall organizational success.

1.7 The Path to Developing Emotional Intelligence

Enhancing Emotional Intelligence (EI) is a lifelong journey that requires dedication, self-awareness, and deliberate practice. By actively engaging in various strategies and techniques, individuals can develop and strengthen their emotional competencies, leading to greater self-awareness, improved relationships, and enhanced overall well-being. Here are some pathways to developing EI:

1. Mindfulness and Self-Reflection

Mindfulness involves paying attention to the present moment with openness, curiosity, and acceptance. It allows individuals to observe their thoughts, emotions, and sensations without judgment, fostering greater self-awareness and emotional regulation. Regular mindfulness practice, such as meditation or deep breathing exercises, can help individuals become more attuned to their internal experiences and cultivate a sense of inner peace and calm.

Anika, a university student, incorporates mindfulness into her daily routine by practicing meditation for a few minutes each morning. Through mindful breathing and body scans, Anika learns to observe her thoughts and emotions without reacting impulsively. This heightened awareness enables her to recognize triggers and manage stress more effectively, ultimately enhancing her emotional resilience and well-being.

2. Empathy Exercises

Empathy is the ability to understand and share the feelings of others, and it is a fundamental aspect of Emotional Intelligence. Practicing empathy exercises, such as perspective-taking and active listening, can help individuals develop greater compassion, understanding, and connection with others. By stepping into someone else's shoes and seeing the world from their perspective, individuals can build stronger relationships and foster empathy in their interactions.

Ahid, a university student, participates in empathy exercises during a communication skills workshop. Through role-playing scenarios and group discussions, Ahid learns to listen attentively to others' perspectives and validate their emotions. These exercises deepen Ahid's empathy skills and help him cultivate more meaningful and supportive relationships with his peers and colleagues.

3. Communication Skills Training

Effective communication is essential for building healthy relationships, resolving conflicts, and expressing oneself authentically. Communication skills training focuses on improving verbal and non-verbal communication, active listening, assertiveness, and conflict resolution skills. By honing these skills, individuals can enhance their ability to express their emotions clearly, understand others' perspectives, and navigate interpersonal interactions with confidence and empathy.

University clubs and organizations, such as debating societies or volunteer groups, offer great opportunities for students to develop their EI through teamwork, public speaking, and community service. By participating in group discussions, presentations, and collaborative projects, students can enhance their communication skills, build empathy, and learn to work effectively with diverse teams. Additionally, volunteering in community service projects allows students to connect with others, practice empathy, and contribute positively to their communities.

4. Seeking Feedback and Support

Feedback from others can provide valuable insights into our strengths and areas for improvement in Emotional Intelligence. Seeking feedback from trusted mentors, colleagues, or friends can help individuals gain a deeper understanding of how their emotions and behaviors impact others and identify areas for growth. Additionally, seeking support from mental health professionals or EI coaches can provide personalized guidance and strategies for developing EI skills.

Anika, a professional, seeks feedback from her colleagues during a team meeting. She asks for specific examples of how her communication style and leadership approach have impacted the team dynamics. By actively listening to their feedback and reflecting on their perspectives, Anika gains valuable insights into her emotional strengths and areas for improvement. She then works with an EI coach to develop personalized strategies for enhancing her leadership skills and fostering a more collaborative and supportive work environment.

CHAPTER TWO

SELF-AWARENESS AND SELF-REGULATION

2.1 Understanding Self-Awareness

Self-awareness is akin to shining a light inward, illuminating the landscape of our emotions, thoughts, and behaviors. It serves as the cornerstone of Emotional Intelligence (EI), the bedrock upon which our ability to navigate the complexities of human interaction is built. At its essence, self-awareness entails a profound recognition of the self — a deep-seated understanding of who we are, what we feel, and why we feel it. In the tapestry of human experience, emotions are the vibrant threads that weave together the fabric of our lives. Self-awareness invites us to explore this rich tapestry, to delve into the depths of our emotional landscape and unearth the intricate patterns that shape our inner world. It empowers us to discern the subtle nuances of our emotions, from the gentle whispers of contentment to the tumultuous waves of sorrow and anger. By tuning into our emotional experiences with openness and curiosity, we gain invaluable insights into the intricacies of our psyche. Yet, self-awareness extends beyond the realm of emotions, encompassing the realm of thought and behavior as well. It beckons us to turn our gaze inward, to examine the tapestry of our thoughts and beliefs with a discerning eye. Through introspection and reflection, we uncover the underlying patterns that govern our cognitive processes, shedding light on the subconscious forces that shape our perceptions of the world. Moreover, self-awareness empowers us to scrutinize our behavioral tendencies with clarity and insight. It prompts us to examine the motives behind our actions, to discern the driving forces that propel us forward or hold us back. By shining a light on the behavioral patterns that govern our interactions with others, we gain a deeper understanding of the impact we have on those around us. In the quest for self-awareness, we embark on a journey of self-discovery — a journey that unfolds gradually, revealing new layers of insight and understanding with each passing day. It is a journey fraught with challenges and obstacles, yet brimming with the promise of growth and transformation. As we navigate the labyrinth of our inner world, we confront our fears and insecurities, our hopes and aspirations, with courage and humility. Developing self-awareness requires courage, vulnerability, and a willingness to embrace the full spectrum of our humanity. It entails confronting the shadowy recesses of our psyche, acknowledging the parts of ourselves that we may prefer to keep hidden from view. Yet, it is through this process of self-exploration that we cultivate a deeper sense of authenticity and integrity, aligning ourselves more closely with our truest selves. Furthermore, self-awareness empowers us to recognize our strengths and weaknesses with clarity and objectivity. It invites us to celebrate our successes and accomplishments, while also acknowledging the areas in which we have room for growth and improvement. By embracing our imperfections with compassion and humility, we create space for growth and self-acceptance, fostering a sense of wholeness and completeness within ourselves. In essence, self-awareness serves as the foundation upon which our capacity for Emotional Intelligence is built. It is the bedrock upon which we cultivate empathy, resilience, and authenticity, enabling us to navigate the complexities of human interaction with grace and wisdom. As we embark on the journey of self-awareness, we embark on a journey of self-discovery — a journey that leads us ever closer to the essence of who we are, and the profound interconnectedness that binds us all.

2.2 Cultivating Self-Regulation

Cultivating self-regulation is akin to mastering the art of taming the wild stallions of our emotions, guiding them with a steady hand and a compassionate heart. It is the ability to harness the tempestuous forces of our inner world and channel them towards constructive ends. Self-regulation is a fundamental aspect of Emotional Intelligence (EI), enabling us to manage our impulses, control our reactions, and make thoughtful decisions in the face of adversity. At its core, self-regulation is about maintaining equilibrium amidst the ebb and flow of life's challenges and uncertainties. It involves staying calm under pressure, resisting the urge to react impulsively, and responding to situations with clarity and composure. Cultivating self-regulation requires cultivating a deep sense of self-awareness — a keen understanding of our emotional triggers, behavioral patterns, and cognitive biases. One of the key pillars of self-regulation is emotional control. Emotions are like the weather patterns of the mind — unpredictable, yet profoundly influential in shaping our thoughts and actions. Cultivating emotional control involves learning to ride the waves of our emotions with grace and resilience, rather than being swept away by them. It requires acknowledging our feelings without judgment, allowing them to flow through us without becoming overwhelmed or consumed by them. Moreover, self-regulation entails managing our impulses and urges with discipline and restraint. It is about pausing to consider the consequences of our actions before acting upon them, weighing the short-term gratification against the long-term consequences. By exercising restraint and impulse control, we can avoid succumbing to the lure of immediate gratification and make decisions that align with our values and goals. Furthermore, self-regulation involves cultivating cognitive control — the ability to regulate our thoughts and attention with focus and clarity. In today's fast-paced world, our attention is constantly bombarded by distractions and stimuli, making it challenging to maintain mental clarity and concentration. Cultivating cognitive control allows us to filter out distractions, stay present in the moment, and direct our attention towards tasks that matter most. Developing self-regulation requires practice, patience, and perseverance. It is a skill that can be honed through intentional effort and mindfulness. Mindfulness practices such as meditation, deep breathing, and body scanning can help cultivate greater self-awareness and emotional control. By observing our thoughts and emotions with curiosity and non-judgmental awareness, we can develop greater resilience in the face of adversity. Moreover, setting goals and creating routines can help reinforce self-regulation habits and promote consistency in our behaviors. By establishing clear objectives and breaking them down into manageable steps, we can create a roadmap for success and stay motivated to persevere towards our goals. Additionally, creating daily rituals and routines can provide structure and stability in our lives, making it easier to maintain self-discipline and resist temptation. Furthermore, developing self-regulation requires cultivating self-compassion and self-acceptance. It is important to acknowledge that we are all human, and we are bound to make mistakes along the way. By treating ourselves with kindness and understanding, we can learn from our failures and setbacks without succumbing to self-criticism or despair. Self-compassion allows us to pick ourselves up, dust ourselves off, and continue moving forward on our journey towards personal growth and fulfillment.

2.3 Recognizing Emotional Triggers

Emotional triggers are the invisible threads that tug at the fabric of our psyche, stirring up a whirlwind of emotions and unleashing a torrent of reactions. They are the catalysts that ignite the flames of our inner world, evoking visceral responses that can range from intense fear and anger to profound sadness and joy. Emotional triggers can manifest in various forms — from seemingly innocuous events or situations to deeply ingrained memories or traumas that lie dormant within our subconscious. Recognizing emotional triggers is essential for cultivating self-awareness and self-regulation, as it allows us to navigate the labyrinth of our inner world with clarity and insight. By shining a light on these hidden triggers, we gain a deeper understanding of the underlying patterns that govern our emotional responses and behavioral tendencies. This awareness empowers us to anticipate and manage our reactions more effectively, enabling us to respond to challenging situations with grace and resilience. One of the first steps in recognizing emotional triggers is cultivating self-awareness — a keen understanding of our thoughts, emotions, and behaviors. Through introspection and reflection, we can begin to unravel the intricate tapestry of our inner world, uncovering the subtle nuances of our emotional landscape. By paying close attention to our emotional reactions in various situations, we can identify recurring patterns or themes that serve as clues to our emotional triggers. Moreover, recognizing emotional triggers requires attunement to the subtle cues and signals that signal their presence. These cues can manifest in various forms — from physical sensations such as a tightening of the chest or a knot in the stomach to cognitive distortions such as black-and-white thinking or catastrophizing. By tuning into these subtle signals, we can become more adept at recognizing when we are being triggered and taking proactive measures to manage our responses. Furthermore, recognizing emotional triggers involves exploring the underlying beliefs, assumptions, and interpretations that fuel our emotional reactions. Our triggers are often rooted in deeply held beliefs or past experiences that shape our perceptions of the world. By interrogating these beliefs with curiosity and openness, we can uncover the hidden drivers behind our emotional responses and challenge them with more adaptive and empowering alternatives. For example, suppose someone experiences intense anxiety whenever they receive criticism or feedback from others. In that case, they may trace this emotional trigger back to a childhood experience of being harshly criticized or ridiculed by a parent or authority figure. By recognizing this trigger and its underlying roots, they can begin to challenge the belief that criticism is inherently threatening or harmful and develop more adaptive coping strategies, such as self-compassion or assertive communication. Moreover, recognizing emotional triggers involves cultivating mindfulness — a present-moment awareness of our thoughts, emotions, and sensations without judgment. Mindfulness practices such as meditation, deep breathing, and body scanning can help us develop greater clarity and insight into our internal experiences, making it easier to identify and manage our triggers. By observing our thoughts and emotions with curiosity and non-judgmental awareness, we can create space between stimulus and response, allowing us to choose how we want to react consciously. Additionally, recognizing emotional triggers requires self-compassion — a kind and understanding attitude towards ourselves, especially in moments of difficulty or distress. It is essential to acknowledge that experiencing emotional triggers is a normal and natural part of the human experience. By treating ourselves with kindness and compassion, we can cultivate resilience and inner strength, enabling us to navigate our triggers with grace and dignity.

2.4 Setting Boundaries

Setting boundaries is akin to drawing a line in the sand, demarcating the contours of our inner landscape and safeguarding our emotional and mental well-being. Boundaries serve as the invisible barriers that define the limits of acceptable behavior and protect our physical, emotional, and mental space. They are the guardian angels that shield us from harm and preserve our sense of self-respect, autonomy, and dignity. At its essence, setting boundaries is about honoring our needs, values, and priorities, and communicating them assertively to others. It is about establishing clear guidelines for how we expect to be treated and upholding those boundaries with firmness and compassion. Setting boundaries empowers us to take ownership of our lives, cultivate healthier relationships, and create space for growth and self-expression. One of the key aspects of setting boundaries is cultivating self-awareness — a deep understanding of our needs, values, and boundaries. Through introspection and reflection, we can identify the aspects of our lives that are non-negotiable and the areas where we are willing to be more flexible. By tuning into our emotions and paying attention to our physical and psychological cues, we can discern when our boundaries are being violated and take proactive steps to assert them. Moreover, setting boundaries requires clarity and assertiveness in communication. It is essential to communicate our boundaries clearly, directly, and respectfully, without resorting to aggression or manipulation. By expressing our needs and preferences assertively, we signal to others that we value ourselves and expect to be treated with respect and consideration. Setting boundaries empowers us to take ownership of our experiences and assert our rights and values in all areas of our lives. Furthermore, setting boundaries involves recognizing and respecting the boundaries of others. It is essential to acknowledge that everyone has their own unique needs, values, and boundaries, and that these may differ from our own. By respecting the boundaries of others, we foster mutual respect and understanding in our relationships, creating a supportive and nurturing environment where everyone feels valued and respected. For example, suppose someone sets a boundary with a friend by expressing their need for alone time and declining an invitation to socialize. In that case, it is essential for the friend to respect that boundary and refrain from pressuring or guilting them into changing their mind. By honoring each other's boundaries, they can cultivate a relationship built on trust, respect, and mutual understanding. Moreover, setting boundaries involves enforcing consequences when our boundaries are violated. It is essential to establish clear consequences for boundary violations and enforce them consistently and assertively. By holding others accountable for their actions and refusing to tolerate behavior that undermines our well-being, we send a clear message that our boundaries are non-negotiable and deserving of respect. Additionally, setting boundaries requires self-compassion and self-care. It is essential to prioritize our well-being and take care of ourselves physically, emotionally, and mentally. By setting boundaries that prioritize our needs and values, we create space for self-care and nourish our relationships with ourselves and others.

2.5 Practicing Self-Compassion

Practicing self-compassion is akin to extending a warm embrace to ourselves in moments of struggle or adversity, offering solace and understanding to the wounded parts of our being. It is the act of turning inward with kindness and acceptance, acknowledging our humanity, flaws, and vulnerabilities, and embracing ourselves with unconditional love and compassion. Self-compassion is not about indulgence or self-pity but rather about recognizing our inherent worthiness and treating ourselves with the same tenderness and care we would offer to a dear friend in need. At its core, self-compassion involves three key elements: self-kindness, common humanity, and mindfulness. Self-kindness is the practice of treating ourselves with warmth, gentleness, and understanding, particularly in moments of pain or difficulty. It entails offering ourselves words of encouragement, comfort, and support, rather than harsh self-criticism or judgment. By cultivating self-kindness, we create a nurturing inner environment that fosters emotional well-being and resilience. Moreover, self-compassion involves recognizing our common humanity — the shared experience of being human and the inevitability of suffering and imperfection. It is about acknowledging that struggle, failure, and pain are universal aspects of the human condition, and that we are not alone in our struggles. By embracing our common humanity, we cultivate a sense of connection and belonging with others, fostering empathy, compassion, and understanding towards ourselves and others. Furthermore, self-compassion entails mindfulness — a present-moment awareness of our thoughts, emotions, and sensations without judgment. Mindfulness allows us to observe our inner experiences with curiosity and openness, rather than getting swept away by them. By cultivating mindfulness, we create space between ourselves and our thoughts and emotions, enabling us to respond to them with clarity and wisdom, rather than reacting impulsively or unconsciously. One of the key benefits of practicing self-compassion is its role in fostering emotional well-being and resilience. Research has shown that self-compassionate individuals tend to experience lower levels of anxiety, depression, and stress, and higher levels of life satisfaction and psychological well-being. By treating ourselves with kindness and understanding, we create a supportive inner environment that promotes emotional healing and growth, enabling us to navigate life's challenges with grace and resilience. Moreover, self-compassion cultivates a sense of interconnectedness with others, fostering empathy, compassion, and understanding towards ourselves and others. When we recognize our shared humanity and embrace ourselves with kindness and acceptance, we create a ripple effect that extends outward, touching the lives of those around us. By treating ourselves with compassion, we model self-care and self-love for others, inspiring them to do the same for themselves and others. Additionally, practicing self-compassion is essential for cultivating a healthy relationship with ourselves and nurturing our overall well-being. When we treat ourselves with kindness and acceptance, we create a foundation of self-worth and self-respect that permeates every aspect of our lives. By acknowledging our worthiness and deservingness of love and compassion, we empower ourselves to pursue our dreams and aspirations with confidence and resilience. Furthermore, self-compassion is a powerful antidote to the inner critic — the critical voice that undermines our confidence and self-esteem. When we respond to our inner critic with self-compassion, we disarm its power and create space for self-acceptance and growth. By offering ourselves kindness and understanding in moments of self-doubt or criticism, we cultivate a sense of inner strength and resilience that enables us to overcome obstacles and pursue our goals with courage and determination.

2.6 Seeking Feedback and Self-Reflection

Seeking feedback and engaging in self-reflection are two interconnected practices that serve as powerful tools for personal and professional development. Together, they form a dynamic duo that empowers us to cultivate self-awareness, refine our skills, and navigate the complexities of life with clarity and intention. Feedback from others serves as a mirror that reflects back to us our strengths, weaknesses, and blind spots. It offers a fresh perspective on our thoughts, behaviors, and actions, shedding light on aspects of ourselves that may have escaped our notice. Whether solicited or unsolicited, feedback provides valuable insights that can help us gain a deeper understanding of our impact on others and the areas in which we have room for growth. Moreover, seeking feedback requires humility, openness, and a willingness to listen and learn from others. It is essential to approach feedback with a growth mindset — a belief that our abilities and talents can be developed through dedication and effort. By embracing feedback as an opportunity for growth and self-improvement, we create space for learning and development, enabling us to reach our full potential. Furthermore, feedback serves as a catalyst for self-reflection — the process of examining our thoughts, emotions, and behaviors with curiosity and openness. Self-reflection invites us to turn inward and explore the deeper layers of our psyche, uncovering the underlying patterns that govern our thoughts and actions. By cultivating self-awareness through self-reflection, we gain greater clarity and insight into our motivations, values, and aspirations. Self-reflection also enables us to identify our triggers, biases, and limiting beliefs that may be holding us back from reaching our full potential. By shining a light on these hidden patterns, we can begin to challenge them with curiosity and compassion, creating space for growth and transformation. Self-reflection empowers us to take ownership of our thoughts and behaviors, enabling us to make more conscious and intentional choices in our lives. Moreover, self-reflection fosters resilience and adaptability in the face of adversity. By examining our experiences with curiosity and openness, we can extract valuable lessons and insights that enable us to bounce back stronger and wiser. Self-reflection allows us to reframe challenges as opportunities for growth and learning, empowering us to overcome obstacles with grace and resilience. In addition to seeking feedback and engaging in self-reflection individually, it is also valuable to cultivate a culture of feedback and reflection within our teams and organizations. By creating space for open and honest communication, we foster a supportive environment where individuals feel empowered to share their perspectives and insights openly. This culture of feedback and reflection enables us to leverage the collective wisdom and expertise of our team members, driving innovation, collaboration, and continuous improvement.

2.7 Conclusion

In the journey of exploring emotional intelligence, we've delved into the intricacies of self-awareness and self-regulation, navigating the labyrinth of our inner world with curiosity and compassion. From understanding the nuances of our emotions to harnessing the tempestuous forces of our inner landscape, we've embarked on a transformative journey towards greater self-awareness and emotional resilience. Self-awareness, the cornerstone of emotional intelligence, invites us to shine a light inward, illuminating the landscape of our emotions, thoughts, and behaviors. It empowers us to recognize our strengths and weaknesses, embrace our imperfections with compassion, and cultivate a deeper understanding of ourselves. Self-regulation, on the other hand, is the art of mastering the wild stallions of our emotions, guiding them with a steady hand and a compassionate heart. It involves maintaining equilibrium amidst life's challenges, resisting the urge to react impulsively, and responding to situations with clarity and composure. Throughout our exploration, we've uncovered the importance of recognizing emotional triggers, setting boundaries, and practicing self-compassion as essential components of emotional well-being. By cultivating mindfulness, embracing our common humanity, and seeking feedback with humility and openness, we've laid the foundation for personal growth and transformation. As we conclude this chapter, let us remember that the journey towards emotional intelligence is not a destination but a continuous process of growth and self-discovery. It requires courage, vulnerability, and a willingness to embrace the full spectrum of our humanity. By cultivating self-awareness, self-regulation, and compassion towards ourselves and others, we empower ourselves to navigate life's challenges with grace and wisdom, fostering deeper connections and a greater sense of fulfillment along the way. May this journey serve as a beacon of inspiration, guiding us towards a life filled with authenticity, resilience, and emotional well-being. As we embark on the path ahead, may we continue to nurture the seeds of emotional intelligence within ourselves and sow the seeds of compassion and understanding in the world around us.

CHAPTER THREE

HARNESSING MOTIVATION AND BUILDING EMPATHY

3.1 Unleashing Intrinsic Motivation

Motivation is a fascinating and multifaceted aspect of human psychology, driving us to pursue our dreams, overcome obstacles, and achieve our goals. At its core, motivation is the force that compels us to act, propelling us forward on our journey through life. While there are many different sources of motivation, ranging from external rewards to internal drives, intrinsic motivation stands out as a particularly powerful and enduring force. Intrinsic motivation refers to the inner desire and passion that fuel our actions and behaviors. Unlike extrinsic motivation, which comes from external sources such as rewards, praise, or recognition, intrinsic motivation arises from within. It is driven by a deep sense of purpose, satisfaction, and fulfillment that comes from engaging in activities that align with our values, interests, and passions. One of the defining characteristics of intrinsic motivation is its sustainability. While external rewards may provide temporary boosts of motivation, they often lose their effectiveness over time. In contrast, intrinsic motivation is self-sustaining, providing a constant source of energy and enthusiasm that propels us forward, even in the face of challenges and setbacks. When we are intrinsically motivated, we are more likely to experience a state of flow – a state of intense focus and immersion in an activity where we lose track of time and become fully absorbed in the present moment. This state of flow is deeply satisfying and fulfilling, fueling our desire to continue engaging in the activity for its own sake, rather than for any external rewards or incentives. Aligning our goals with our values and aspirations is essential for unleashing intrinsic motivation. When our goals are meaningful and personally significant, we are more likely to feel a sense of purpose and passion that drives us to take action. For example, someone who is passionate about environmental conservation may feel intrinsically motivated to volunteer for clean-up efforts or advocate for policy change. Moreover, intrinsic motivation is closely linked to autonomy – the sense of control and agency we have over our actions and decisions. When we feel that we have the freedom to pursue our goals in a way that aligns with our values and interests, we are more likely to experience a sense of intrinsic motivation. This is why autonomy is a key component of motivation in educational settings, where students are encouraged to take ownership of their learning and pursue topics that interest them. Another important factor that influences intrinsic motivation is mastery – the sense of progress and improvement we experience when we engage in challenging activities. When we are able to see tangible results and improvements in our skills and abilities over time, we are more likely to feel motivated to continue putting in effort and persevering in the face of difficulties. Intrinsic motivation is not only important for personal fulfillment and well-being but also for achieving success in various domains of life, including education, work, and relationships. When we are intrinsically motivated, we are more likely to set ambitious goals, persist in the face of obstacles, and ultimately achieve our full potential.

3.2 Setting Meaningful Goals

Setting meaningful goals is a pivotal aspect of personal and professional development, serving as a roadmap that guides our actions and propels us toward our desired outcomes. While the act of goal-setting itself may seem straightforward, the process of crafting goals that resonate deeply with our values, passions, and aspirations requires careful consideration and introspection. Meaningful goals are those that inspire us to stretch beyond our comfort zones, challenge ourselves, and strive for excellence in pursuit of our dreams. The first step in setting meaningful goals is to clarify our values and priorities. Our values represent the principles and ideals that are most important to us, guiding our decisions and actions in life. By identifying our core values, we gain insight into what truly matters to us and can align our goals accordingly. For example, if one of our core values is environmental sustainability, we may set goals related to reducing our carbon footprint, promoting renewable energy, or supporting conservation efforts. Once we have clarified our values, the next step is to identify our passions and interests. Our passions are the activities, hobbies, or causes that ignite our enthusiasm and bring us joy. By tapping into our passions, we can set goals that resonate deeply with our intrinsic motivations, fueling our drive and commitment to succeed. For instance, if we are passionate about music, we may set goals to learn a new instrument, compose a song, or perform at a local venue. After clarifying our values and passions, we can begin to set specific, measurable, achievable, relevant, and time-bound (SMART) goals that align with our aspirations. SMART goals provide a clear framework for defining our objectives and tracking our progress toward achieving them. For example, instead of setting a vague goal like "get in shape," we might set a SMART goal like "run a 5K race in under 30 minutes by the end of the year." In addition to being SMART, meaningful goals are also challenging yet attainable. Setting goals that push us outside of our comfort zones and require effort and dedication to achieve can inspire us to grow and develop in meaningful ways. However, it's essential to strike a balance between ambition and feasibility to prevent feelings of overwhelm or discouragement. Breaking larger goals down into smaller, more manageable milestones can help make them feel more achievable and keep us motivated along the way. Furthermore, meaningful goals are aligned with our long-term vision for ourselves and contribute to our overall sense of purpose and fulfillment. When our goals are congruent with our larger aspirations and life trajectory, we are more likely to stay committed and motivated, even when faced with obstacles or setbacks. Regularly revisiting our goals and reflecting on how they align with our values and aspirations can help ensure that we stay on track and make adjustments as needed.

3.3 Fostering Resilience

Resilience, often regarded as the cornerstone of personal and professional success, is a dynamic trait that empowers individuals to navigate life's inevitable challenges and setbacks with grace and fortitude. It is the ability to adapt, bounce back, and thrive in the face of adversity, adversity, uncertainty, and change. While resilience is often associated with extraordinary feats of strength and endurance, it is a skill that can be cultivated and nurtured over time through intentional effort and practice. At its core, resilience is rooted in a mindset characterized by optimism, flexibility, and perseverance. It involves viewing setbacks and failures not as insurmountable obstacles but as opportunities for growth and learning. Resilient individuals possess a sense of agency and empowerment, recognizing that they have the ability to influence and shape their circumstances, even in the face of adversity. They embrace challenges with a spirit of curiosity and openness, knowing that each obstacle presents a chance to learn, adapt, and evolve. One of the key components of resilience is emotional regulation — the ability to manage and navigate difficult emotions effectively. Resilient individuals are adept at acknowledging their feelings without being overwhelmed by them, allowing themselves to experience and process emotions such as sadness, anger, or fear without becoming consumed by them. By cultivating emotional regulation, individuals can maintain a sense of balance and equanimity even in the midst of life's storms, enabling them to respond to challenges with clarity and composure. Moreover, resilience is closely tied to the concept of cognitive flexibility — the ability to adapt one's thinking and perspective in response to changing circumstances. Resilient individuals are skilled at reframing challenges and setbacks in a more positive and empowering light, seeing them as opportunities for growth and development rather than as threats to their well-being. They are open-minded and adaptable, willing to explore new possibilities and consider alternative solutions when faced with obstacles. Additionally, resilience is fostered through a strong sense of social support and connection. Resilient individuals cultivate meaningful relationships with others, relying on their support and encouragement during times of difficulty. They are not afraid to seek help when needed, recognizing that vulnerability is a sign of strength rather than weakness. By surrounding themselves with a supportive network of friends, family, and colleagues, resilient individuals can draw strength and inspiration from others, knowing that they are not alone in their journey. Furthermore, resilience is nurtured through self-care and self-compassion. Resilient individuals prioritize their physical, emotional, and mental well-being, engaging in activities that nourish and replenish their energy reserves. They practice self-compassion, treating themselves with kindness and understanding, especially in moments of struggle or failure. By prioritizing self-care and self-compassion, resilient individuals can replenish their inner resources and maintain a sense of balance and equilibrium, even in the face of adversity.

3.4 Cultivating Empathy

Empathy, often described as the ability to understand and share the feelings of others, is a fundamental aspect of human interaction that plays a crucial role in fostering meaningful relationships and nurturing a sense of connection and belonging. It involves not only recognizing and acknowledging the emotions of others but also responding to them with kindness, compassion, and understanding. Cultivating empathy requires a willingness to step outside of our own perspective and immerse ourselves in the experiences and emotions of others, fostering a deeper sense of connection and empathy that transcends individual differences and unites us in our shared humanity. At its core, empathy is rooted in the capacity for emotional resonance — the ability to attune ourselves to the emotions of others and respond to them with sensitivity and compassion. This involves not only recognizing and validating the feelings of others but also expressing genuine concern and care for their well-being. Empathetic individuals possess a heightened sensitivity to the emotional cues and signals of others, allowing them to pick up on subtle nuances and expressions that may go unnoticed by others. By tuning into these emotional cues with empathy and compassion, individuals can create a safe and supportive space for others to express themselves authentically and openly. Moreover, empathy involves perspective-taking — the ability to step into the shoes of another person and see the world from their perspective. This requires a willingness to set aside our own biases, assumptions, and judgments and approach others with an open mind and heart. By cultivating curiosity and humility, we can gain a deeper understanding of the experiences and perspectives of others, fostering empathy and compassion that transcends individual differences and fosters a sense of connection and belonging. Furthermore, empathy involves active listening — the art of listening deeply and attentively to others' experiences and perspectives without judgment or interruption. This involves not only hearing the words that are spoken but also paying attention to the underlying emotions and needs that may lie beneath the surface. By practicing active listening with empathy and compassion, individuals can create a space for others to feel heard, validated, and understood, fostering a sense of connection and trust that forms the foundation of meaningful relationships. Additionally, empathy involves emotional regulation — the ability to manage and navigate our own emotions effectively in response to the emotions of others. This involves recognizing and acknowledging our own emotional responses without becoming overwhelmed or consumed by them, allowing us to respond to others' emotions with clarity and compassion. By cultivating emotional regulation, individuals can maintain a sense of balance and equanimity in their interactions with others, fostering empathy and compassion that is grounded in a deep sense of self-awareness and self-compassion.

3.5 Nurturing Emotional Intelligence

Emotional intelligence (EI) serves as the cornerstone of our ability to navigate the complexities of human interaction and foster meaningful relationships both personally and professionally. It encompasses a range of skills and abilities that enable us to recognize, understand, and manage our own emotions, as well as the emotions of others. Nurturing emotional intelligence involves cultivating self-awareness, self-regulation, empathy, and social skills, which collectively contribute to our overall well-being and interpersonal effectiveness. At its core, self-awareness forms the foundation of emotional intelligence. It involves having a deep understanding of our own emotions, thoughts, and behaviors, as well as their impact on ourselves and others. By cultivating self-awareness, we gain insight into our strengths, weaknesses, values, and priorities, enabling us to make more informed decisions and navigate life's challenges with greater ease. Self-awareness also allows us to recognize our emotional triggers and patterns of behavior, empowering us to respond to situations with clarity and composure rather than reacting impulsively. Self-regulation is another key component of emotional intelligence. It involves managing our emotions, impulses, and behaviors in a constructive and adaptive manner, particularly in times of stress or adversity. By developing self-regulation skills, we can remain calm and composed in challenging situations, resist the urge to react impulsively, and make thoughtful decisions that align with our values and goals. Self-regulation also enables us to maintain a sense of balance and equanimity in our interactions with others, fostering trust, respect, and mutual understanding. Empathy is a crucial aspect of emotional intelligence that involves understanding and sharing the feelings of others. It requires us to put ourselves in someone else's shoes, to see the world from their perspective, and to respond with kindness and compassion. Cultivating empathy allows us to connect with others on a deeper level, fostering trust, understanding, and mutual respect in our relationships. Empathetic individuals are better able to recognize and respond to the emotional needs of others, creating a supportive and nurturing environment that promotes emotional well-being and interpersonal harmony. Social skills encompass a range of abilities that enable us to interact effectively with others, build and maintain relationships, and navigate social situations with ease. These skills include communication, conflict resolution, negotiation, and collaboration, among others. By honing our social skills, we can foster positive and constructive relationships with colleagues, friends, and family members, enhancing our personal and professional success. Socially skilled individuals are adept at navigating diverse social contexts, adapting their communication style to suit the needs and preferences of others, and resolving conflicts and disagreements in a constructive and respectful manner.

3.6 Building Empathetic Leadership

Empathetic leadership represents a paradigm shift in the way we approach leadership, emphasizing compassion, understanding, and authenticity in our interactions with others. It is a leadership style that prioritizes the well-being and growth of individuals, fostering a supportive and inclusive environment where everyone feels valued, respected, and empowered to thrive. Building empathetic leadership involves cultivating a range of skills and qualities that enable us to connect deeply with others, inspire trust, and foster collaboration and cooperation within our teams and organizations. At the heart of empathetic leadership lies empathy — the ability to understand and share the feelings of others. Empathetic leaders possess a keen awareness of the emotions, needs, and perspectives of their team members, allowing them to respond with sensitivity and compassion to their concerns and challenges. By demonstrating empathy in their interactions, leaders create a safe and supportive space where individuals feel heard, understood, and valued, fostering trust and psychological safety within the team. Humility is another key characteristic of empathetic leadership. Humble leaders are open-minded, approachable, and willing to admit their mistakes and limitations. They recognize that leadership is not about exerting power or authority but rather about serving others and empowering them to reach their full potential. By embracing humility, leaders create a culture of openness and transparency where individuals feel comfortable expressing their ideas and opinions without fear of judgment or retribution. Integrity is essential to empathetic leadership. Leaders who act with integrity demonstrate honesty, fairness, and consistency in their words and actions. They uphold high ethical standards and lead by example, inspiring trust and confidence in their team members. By demonstrating integrity in their leadership, they create a culture of accountability and integrity within the organization, where individuals are committed to doing the right thing even when no one is watching. Effective communication is another critical skill for empathetic leadership. Empathetic leaders are skilled communicators who listen actively, communicate clearly, and convey empathy and understanding in their interactions. They take the time to understand the perspectives and concerns of their team members, seeking feedback and input to inform their decisions and actions. By fostering open and transparent communication, leaders create a culture of trust and collaboration, where individuals feel empowered to contribute their ideas and insights to the team. Empathetic leaders also prioritize the well-being and growth of their team members. They invest time and resources in developing their skills and capabilities, providing mentorship, guidance, and support to help them achieve their goals. By demonstrating a genuine concern for the personal and professional development of their team members, leaders foster a culture of learning and growth within the organization, where individuals are motivated to continuously improve and innovate.

3.7 Embracing Diversity and Inclusion

Embracing diversity and inclusion is not only a moral imperative but also a strategic advantage in today's interconnected and globalized world. Diversity encompasses the infinite spectrum of human differences, including but not limited to race, ethnicity, gender, age, sexual orientation, disability, religion, socioeconomic status, and cultural background. Inclusion, on the other hand, refers to the deliberate and proactive efforts to create a sense of belonging and acceptance for all individuals, regardless of their differences. At its core, embracing diversity and inclusion is about recognizing the inherent value and dignity of every individual and creating a culture that celebrates and honors their unique identities and contributions. It is about moving beyond tolerance and mere representation to actively fostering an environment where everyone feels valued, respected, and empowered to bring their authentic selves to the table. One of the key benefits of embracing diversity and inclusion is the fostering of creativity and innovation. Research has consistently shown that diverse teams are more creative and innovative than homogenous ones. When individuals from different backgrounds, perspectives, and experiences come together, they bring a diverse range of ideas, insights, and approaches to problem-solving, leading to more robust and innovative solutions. By embracing diversity and creating an inclusive environment where everyone's voice is heard and valued, organizations can unlock the full creative potential of their teams, driving innovation and competitive advantage. Moreover, embracing diversity and inclusion fosters resilience and adaptability in the face of change and uncertainty. In today's rapidly changing and interconnected world, organizations must be agile and flexible to navigate complex challenges and seize emerging opportunities. By embracing diversity and inclusion, organizations cultivate a culture of openness, collaboration, and mutual respect, where individuals are encouraged to share their perspectives, take risks, and challenge the status quo. This culture of inclusivity enables organizations to adapt quickly to changing circumstances, harnessing the collective wisdom and creativity of their diverse workforce to drive positive change and innovation. Furthermore, embracing diversity and inclusion is essential for attracting and retaining top talent. In today's competitive labor market, employees are increasingly prioritizing diversity and inclusion when evaluating potential employers. Organizations that prioritize diversity and create an inclusive workplace culture are more likely to attract and retain top talent from diverse backgrounds. By fostering a culture of belonging and empowerment, organizations can create a positive and supportive work environment where employees feel valued, respected, and motivated to perform at their best. Embracing diversity and inclusion also has a positive impact on organizational performance and financial success. Research has shown that companies with diverse leadership teams and inclusive workplace cultures are more likely to outperform their peers financially. By embracing diversity and inclusion, organizations can tap into new markets, better understand the needs and preferences of diverse customer segments, and drive innovation and growth. Moreover, diverse teams are better equipped to anticipate and respond to the needs of an increasingly diverse and global customer base, positioning organizations for long-term success in today's competitive marketplace.

CHAPTER FOUR

ENHANCING SOCIAL SKILLS

4.1 Understanding the Importance of Social Skills

Social skills are an essential aspect of human interaction, shaping our ability to navigate the complexities of social dynamics, communicate effectively, and build meaningful relationships. In today's interconnected world, where success often relies on our ability to connect with others, the importance of honing our social skills cannot be overstated. Whether in personal or professional settings, strong social skills serve as the cornerstone of our ability to interact with authenticity, empathy, and confidence. One of the primary functions of social skills is to facilitate effective communication. Communication is the bedrock of human interaction, allowing us to convey our thoughts, feelings, and intentions to others. Strong social skills enable us to express ourselves clearly and assertively, ensuring that our message is understood and received as intended. Moreover, effective communication involves not only speaking but also active listening, allowing us to understand and empathize with others' perspectives, needs, and emotions. By honing our communication skills, we can foster understanding, collaboration, and connection in our interactions with others. Furthermore, social skills play a crucial role in facilitating collaboration and teamwork. In today's interconnected and interdependent world, many endeavors require individuals to work together towards a common goal. Strong social skills enable us to collaborate effectively with others, leveraging our collective strengths and talents to achieve shared objectives. By fostering open communication, mutual respect, and trust, we can create a supportive and inclusive environment where everyone feels valued and empowered to contribute their best. Additionally, social skills are vital for building and maintaining positive relationships. Relationships are the foundation of human connection, providing us with a sense of belonging, support, and fulfillment. Strong social skills enable us to build rapport, establish trust, and foster connection with others. By demonstrating empathy, kindness, and authenticity in our interactions, we can cultivate meaningful relationships that enrich our lives and bring us joy and fulfillment. Moreover, social skills play a crucial role in navigating the complexities of interpersonal dynamics, allowing us to resolve conflicts, manage differences, and build bridges of understanding and connection. In personal settings, social skills are essential for forming and maintaining friendships, romantic relationships, and familial bonds. Strong social skills enable us to connect with others on a deeper level, share experiences and emotions, and provide support and companionship. By demonstrating empathy, compassion, and active listening, we can strengthen our relationships and create lasting bonds based on trust and mutual respect. In professional settings, social skills are equally important for success and advancement. Whether in leadership roles, team environments, or client-facing positions, strong social skills enable us to communicate effectively, collaborate productively, and build strong professional networks. By demonstrating professionalism, emotional intelligence, and interpersonal competence, we can enhance our credibility, influence, and impact in the workplace.

4.2 Effective Communication

Effective communication is a fundamental skill that underpins successful interactions in both personal and professional contexts. It encompasses a broad range of verbal and nonverbal behaviors that enable individuals to convey their thoughts, feelings, and intentions clearly and accurately. Mastering the art of effective communication is essential for building strong relationships, resolving conflicts, and achieving shared goals. By honing our communication skills, we can foster understanding, collaboration, and connection with others. At its core, effective communication involves the ability to express oneself clearly and assertively. This includes articulating thoughts and ideas in a concise and coherent manner, using language that is appropriate for the audience and context. Clarity in communication ensures that the intended message is understood by the recipient, minimizing the risk of misunderstandings or misinterpretations. Moreover, assertiveness in communication involves expressing one's needs, preferences, and boundaries with confidence and respect, without resorting to aggression or passive-aggressiveness. In addition to verbal communication, nonverbal cues such as body language, facial expressions, and tone of voice play a crucial role in effective communication. Nonverbal communication provides important context and nuance to the spoken word, conveying emotions, attitudes, and intentions that may not be explicitly stated. For example, a warm smile and open posture can signal friendliness and approachability, while crossed arms and furrowed brows may indicate defensiveness or discomfort. By paying attention to both verbal and nonverbal cues, communicators can ensure that their message is congruent and impactful. Active listening is another key component of effective communication. Active listening involves not only hearing the words spoken by the speaker but also paying attention to their tone, body language, and underlying emotions. It requires giving the speaker our full attention, refraining from interrupting or formulating responses prematurely. Instead, active listeners strive to understand the speaker's perspective, asking clarifying questions and paraphrasing their message to ensure comprehension. By demonstrating empathy and validation, active listeners create a supportive environment that encourages open and honest communication. Moreover, effective communication involves adapting one's communication style to suit the preferences and needs of the audience. Different individuals may have varying communication styles, preferences, and cultural backgrounds that influence how they send and receive messages. Skilled communicators are adept at flexing their communication style to accommodate these differences, adjusting their tone, language, and delivery to maximize clarity and receptivity. By tailoring their message to the audience, communicators can enhance understanding and rapport, fostering positive relationships and collaboration. Furthermore, effective communication is characterized by mutual respect and empathy. Respectful communication involves treating others with dignity and consideration, regardless of differences in opinion or background. It entails listening actively, refraining from judgment or criticism, and acknowledging the validity of others' perspectives. Empathetic communication involves demonstrating understanding and compassion towards others' emotions and experiences, validating their feelings and offering support when needed. By practicing respectful and empathetic communication, individuals can build trust, strengthen relationships, and foster a positive and supportive social environment.

4.3 Active Listening

Active listening is a foundational skill in effective communication, crucial for establishing rapport, understanding others' perspectives, and building strong relationships. It goes beyond simply hearing words; it involves fully engaging with the speaker, both verbally and nonverbally, to comprehend not just what they are saying, but also why they are saying it and how they feel about it. Active listening requires attention, empathy, and a genuine desire to understand the speaker's thoughts, feelings, and intentions. At its core, active listening involves giving the speaker our full attention and being fully present in the moment. This means minimizing distractions, such as putting away electronic devices or mentally preparing responses while the speaker is talking. By maintaining eye contact, nodding occasionally, and providing other nonverbal cues of engagement, we signal to the speaker that we are actively listening and interested in what they have to say. Furthermore, active listening entails listening with empathy and openness. Empathetic listening involves not only understanding the content of the speaker's message but also recognizing and validating their emotions. It requires putting ourselves in the speaker's shoes, imagining how we would feel in their situation, and responding with compassion and understanding. By acknowledging the speaker's emotions and showing empathy, we create a supportive and validating environment that encourages them to express themselves openly and honestly. In addition to empathy, active listening involves asking clarifying questions and paraphrasing the speaker's message to ensure understanding. Clarifying questions seek to fill in gaps in our understanding or gather additional information about the speaker's thoughts or feelings. Paraphrasing involves summarizing the speaker's message in our own words, reflecting back what we heard to confirm accuracy and demonstrate active engagement. By seeking clarification and paraphrasing, we demonstrate our commitment to understanding the speaker's perspective and avoid misinterpretations or misunderstandings. Moreover, active listening requires suspending judgment and refraining from interrupting or interjecting prematurely. It involves allowing the speaker to express themselves fully without feeling rushed or pressured. By giving the speaker space to share their thoughts and feelings uninterrupted, we signal our respect for their autonomy and validate their experiences. This creates a safe and supportive environment that encourages open and honest communication. Active listening is especially valuable in conflict resolution and negotiation, where emotions may run high, and miscommunications can escalate tensions. By listening actively and empathetically, we can de-escalate conflicts, build trust, and find common ground with others. Active listening allows us to uncover underlying concerns or interests, identify areas of agreement, and work collaboratively towards mutually beneficial solutions. Furthermore, active listening is essential for building strong relationships, both personally and professionally. By demonstrating genuine interest and concern for others' thoughts and feelings, we foster trust, respect, and rapport. Active listening enables us to build deeper connections with others, strengthen existing relationships, and forge new ones based on mutual understanding and empathy. In professional settings, active listening can enhance teamwork, collaboration, and leadership effectiveness by fostering open communication, boosting morale, and promoting a positive organizational culture.

4.4 Empathy and Perspective-Taking

Empathy and perspective-taking are essential components of emotional intelligence, enabling us to connect with others on a deeper level, understand their experiences, and build stronger, more meaningful relationships. While closely related, empathy and perspective-taking encompass distinct aspects of understanding and relating to others, each contributing to our ability to navigate social interactions with sensitivity and insight. Empathy is the capacity to recognize and share the feelings of others, to vicariously experience their emotions as if they were our own. It involves not only understanding the emotions someone else is experiencing but also responding with compassion and concern. Empathy requires emotional attunement and sensitivity to others' cues, such as facial expressions, body language, and tone of voice. By tuning into these cues and recognizing the underlying emotions they convey, we can empathize with others' experiences and validate their feelings. Perspective-taking, on the other hand, involves stepping outside of our own experiences and viewpoints to see the world from another person's perspective. It requires imagining ourselves in their shoes, considering their thoughts, feelings, and motivations, and understanding how their unique experiences and background shape their perceptions of the world. Perspective-taking involves cognitive empathy, the ability to understand someone else's perspective intellectually, as well as emotional empathy, the ability to share in their emotional experience. Cultivating empathy and perspective-taking begins with a willingness to engage with others with an open mind and heart. It requires curiosity, humility, and a genuine interest in understanding others' experiences and perspectives. By approaching interactions with empathy and curiosity, we create space for connection and mutual understanding, fostering trust, respect, and rapport. One way to cultivate empathy and perspective-taking is through active listening. By listening attentively and empathetically to others' stories, concerns, and experiences, we can gain insight into their thoughts, feelings, and perspectives. Asking open-ended questions and expressing genuine curiosity about others' experiences can deepen our understanding and empathy, allowing us to connect with them on a deeper level. Another strategy for developing empathy and perspective-taking is practicing perspective-switching. This involves intentionally shifting our focus from our own experiences and viewpoints to those of others. For example, we can imagine how we would feel or react in a given situation if we were in someone else's shoes. By practicing perspective-switching, we can broaden our understanding of different perspectives and cultivate empathy for others' experiences. Moreover, exposure to diverse perspectives and experiences can enhance empathy and perspective-taking by challenging our assumptions and expanding our worldview. Engaging with people from different backgrounds, cultures, and life experiences exposes us to a range of perspectives and allows us to see the world through different lenses. By seeking out diverse perspectives and actively listening to others' stories, we can broaden our understanding of human experiences and foster empathy and connection across differences.

4.5 Conflict Resolution

Conflict resolution is a vital skill in both personal and professional contexts, as conflicts inevitably arise in any relationship or group dynamic. Whether it's a disagreement between friends, colleagues, or family members, how we navigate conflict can determine the health and longevity of our relationships. Effective conflict resolution involves a combination of communication, negotiation, empathy, and problem-solving skills to address differences and reach mutually satisfactory resolutions. Communication lies at the heart of effective conflict resolution. Clear and open communication enables parties involved in a conflict to express their concerns, needs, and perspectives in a respectful and constructive manner. By actively listening to each other's viewpoints without interrupting or becoming defensive, individuals can gain a deeper understanding of the underlying issues and emotions driving the conflict. Moreover, using "I" statements to express feelings and observations can help avoid blame and defensiveness, fostering a more collaborative atmosphere conducive to resolution. Active listening is a key component of effective communication in conflict resolution. It involves not only hearing the words spoken but also understanding the emotions and underlying needs behind them. By listening attentively and empathetically to each other's concerns, individuals can demonstrate respect and validation for their perspectives, paving the way for productive dialogue and problem-solving. Empathy plays a crucial role in conflict resolution by allowing individuals to understand and empathize with each other's feelings and experiences. By putting themselves in the other person's shoes and considering their perspective, individuals can develop empathy and compassion, which can defuse tensions and facilitate understanding. Empathetic responses, such as acknowledging the other person's feelings and validating their experiences, can help de-escalate conflicts and create a sense of connection and rapport. Negotiation is another essential skill in conflict resolution, as it involves finding mutually acceptable solutions to address the underlying issues and interests of all parties involved. Effective negotiation requires creativity, flexibility, and a willingness to compromise. By exploring various options and alternatives together, individuals can work collaboratively to find win-win solutions that meet everyone's needs and interests to some extent. Problem-solving skills are critical in conflict resolution, as they enable individuals to identify the root causes of the conflict and brainstorm potential solutions. By focusing on shared goals and interests rather than on positions or demands, individuals can work together to generate creative solutions that address the underlying issues effectively. Moreover, breaking down complex problems into smaller, manageable steps can make the resolution process more manageable and achievable. Maintaining a constructive and respectful tone throughout the conflict resolution process is essential for fostering trust and collaboration. Avoiding personal attacks, blame, and criticism can help keep the conversation focused on the issues at hand and prevent escalation. Additionally, acknowledging and appreciating each other's efforts and contributions towards finding a resolution can help build goodwill and strengthen relationships in the long run.

4.6 Building and Maintaining Relationships

Building and maintaining relationships is a multifaceted process that involves various skills, attitudes, and behaviors. It encompasses not only forming new connections but also nurturing existing ones to ensure they remain strong and fulfilling over time. Effective relationship-building requires authenticity, empathy, trust, communication, and effort to cultivate meaningful connections with others. Authenticity is the foundation of genuine relationships. Being authentic means being true to oneself, expressing thoughts, feelings, and values honestly and transparently. Authenticity fosters trust and mutual respect in relationships, as others appreciate sincerity and genuineness. When individuals are authentic in their interactions, they create an environment where people feel safe to be themselves and express their true thoughts and emotions without fear of judgment. Empathy is another crucial component of building and maintaining relationships. Empathy involves understanding and sharing the feelings of others, putting oneself in their shoes, and responding with compassion and kindness. By empathizing with others' experiences and emotions, individuals can strengthen their connections, build rapport, and foster mutual understanding and support. Empathy enhances communication, deepens emotional bonds, and promotes trust and intimacy in relationships. Trust is essential for the foundation of any healthy relationship. Trust is built over time through consistent and reliable behavior, honesty, integrity, and respect for boundaries. When individuals trust each other, they feel secure and confident in their interactions, knowing they can rely on each other and confide in one another without fear of betrayal or judgment. Building trust requires transparency, consistency, and follow-through in actions and words, demonstrating reliability and accountability. Communication plays a pivotal role in building and maintaining relationships. Effective communication involves both verbal and nonverbal cues, active listening, empathy, and clarity in expressing thoughts and feelings. By communicating openly and honestly, individuals can share their thoughts, emotions, and needs with others, resolve conflicts, and build deeper connections. Active listening, in particular, is essential for understanding others' perspectives, validating their experiences, and fostering mutual respect and understanding. Effort and investment are necessary to build and maintain relationships. Relationships require time, attention, and care to flourish and grow. Individuals must prioritize their relationships, make time for meaningful interactions, and show appreciation and gratitude for the people in their lives. Small gestures of kindness, such as checking in on a friend, offering support during difficult times, or celebrating achievements together, can strengthen bonds and create lasting memories. Building and maintaining relationships also involve navigating challenges and conflicts that arise. Conflict resolution skills, including communication, negotiation, empathy, and problem-solving, are essential for addressing disagreements constructively and preserving the integrity of the relationship. By approaching conflicts with empathy, patience, and a willingness to listen and compromise, individuals can resolve differences and strengthen their connections. Moreover, building and maintaining relationships require adaptability and flexibility to accommodate changes and transitions over time. Individuals must be willing to adapt to evolving circumstances, such as life changes, geographical relocations, or career shifts, while maintaining their connections and nurturing their relationships. Flexibility and resilience enable individuals to navigate challenges and transitions together, strengthening their bonds and deepening their connections.

4.7 Networking and Relationship-Building in Professional Settings

Networking and relationship-building in professional settings are integral components of career development and advancement. These skills enable individuals to establish connections, foster collaborations, and access opportunities that contribute to their professional growth and success. Effective networking goes beyond merely collecting business cards or making superficial connections; it involves building authentic relationships based on mutual trust, respect, and reciprocity. By cultivating a strong professional network, individuals can enhance their visibility, expand their knowledge base, and gain access to valuable resources and support. Authenticity is key to successful networking in professional settings. Authentic networking involves being genuine, sincere, and transparent in interactions with others. Rather than focusing solely on self-promotion or personal gain, authentic networkers prioritize building meaningful connections and offering value to others. Authenticity fosters trust and credibility, making it easier to establish rapport and form lasting relationships within professional circles. Curiosity and openness are also essential qualities for effective networking. Approaching networking with a curious mindset enables individuals to learn from others, explore new ideas, and gain diverse perspectives. By showing genuine interest in others' work, experiences, and perspectives, individuals can initiate meaningful conversations and establish connections based on shared interests and goals. Openness to new opportunities and experiences expands one's professional horizons and facilitates the discovery of potential collaborations or career pathways. Networking is not solely about what one can gain from others but also about what one can contribute to the professional community. Giving back to one's network by offering support, expertise, or resources demonstrates generosity and fosters reciprocity within professional relationships. By actively contributing to the success of others and helping them achieve their goals, individuals strengthen their professional reputation and build a network of allies and advocates who are invested in their success. Building trust is crucial for effective networking and relationship-building in professional settings. Trust forms the foundation of strong professional relationships and enables individuals to collaborate, share ideas, and pursue common objectives with confidence. Trust is cultivated through consistent communication, reliability, integrity, and a commitment to follow through on commitments and promises. By demonstrating trustworthiness and reliability in interactions with others, individuals can earn the respect and confidence of their peers and colleagues, paving the way for meaningful collaborations and opportunities. Effective communication skills are essential for successful networking and relationship-building in professional settings. Clear, concise, and compelling communication enables individuals to articulate their goals, share their expertise, and convey their value proposition effectively. Effective communicators listen actively, ask insightful questions, and tailor their messages to the needs and interests of their audience. By mastering the art of communication, individuals can build rapport, convey credibility, and leave a positive impression on others within their professional network. Strategic networking involves identifying and engaging with key stakeholders, influencers, and decision-makers within one's industry or field. By strategically targeting individuals or groups who can offer valuable insights, connections, or opportunities, individuals can maximize the impact of their networking efforts and accelerate their career progression. Strategic networking involves researching industry events, conferences, or professional organizations, and proactively seeking out opportunities to connect with relevant contacts and expand one's network. Networking and relationship-building in professional settings require persistence, patience, and a long-term perspective. Building meaningful connections takes time and effort, and it is essential to nurture relationships over time through regular communication, follow-up, and engagement. Networking is not a one-time activity but an ongoing process of relationship cultivation and maintenance. By investing in the cultivation of authentic, mutually beneficial relationships, individuals can leverage their professional network to support their career aspirations and achieve long-term success.

CHAPTER FIVE

Applying Emotional Intelligence for Success

5.1 Leveraging Self-Awareness

Self-awareness is like holding a mirror up to our inner selves, reflecting back our thoughts, emotions, and behaviors with clarity and honesty. It forms the bedrock upon which emotional intelligence is built, providing us with the foundation to navigate the complexities of life with insight and understanding. By leveraging self-awareness, individuals can unlock a treasure trove of insights into their inner workings, enabling them to make informed decisions, build meaningful relationships, and achieve their goals. At its core, self-awareness is about knowing oneself deeply — understanding our strengths, weaknesses, values, and motivations. It involves a willingness to explore our inner landscape with curiosity and openness, shining a light into the darkest corners of our psyche. Through introspection and self-reflection, we gain clarity about who we are and what drives us, empowering us to align our actions with our values and aspirations. One of the key benefits of self-awareness is its ability to help us identify our emotional triggers. Emotional triggers are like landmines buried within our psyche, waiting to detonate when activated by certain events or circumstances. By recognizing our emotional triggers, we can anticipate our emotional responses and choose how to react consciously. For example, if public speaking triggers feelings of anxiety, self-awareness enables us to develop coping strategies such as deep breathing or positive self-talk to manage our anxiety effectively. Moreover, self-awareness enables us to regulate our emotions more effectively. Emotions are like waves, ebbing and flowing with the tides of life. Self-awareness allows us to ride these waves with grace and resilience, rather than being swept away by them. By tuning into our emotional experiences with mindfulness and non-judgmental awareness, we can respond to them in ways that are adaptive and constructive. For instance, if we notice feelings of anger arising during a disagreement, self-awareness empowers us to pause, take a deep breath, and respond calmly and assertively instead of reacting impulsively. Self-awareness also fosters resilience in the face of adversity. Life is full of challenges and setbacks, but how we perceive and respond to these challenges can make all the difference. By cultivating self-awareness, we develop the ability to see challenges as opportunities for growth and learning, rather than insurmountable obstacles. We can recognize our patterns of thinking and behavior that may be holding us back and choose to respond to adversity with courage and determination. Self-awareness helps us bounce back from setbacks stronger and more resilient than before. In the realm of personal and professional development, self-awareness is an invaluable tool for growth. It enables us to identify our areas for improvement and take proactive steps to address them. Whether it's seeking feedback from others, enrolling in training programs, or working with a coach or mentor, self-awareness empowers us to invest in our personal and professional growth effectively. By embracing self-awareness as a lifelong journey of discovery, we can continuously evolve and adapt to the ever-changing landscape of life.

5.2 Harnessing Self-Regulation

Self-regulation is the secret ingredient that empowers individuals to navigate life's turbulent waters with grace and resilience. It is the ability to steer the ship of one's emotions, impulses, and behaviors amidst the stormiest of seas, guiding it towards calmer shores. Harnessing self-regulation is not just about controlling our reactions in the heat of the moment; it's about cultivating a deeper sense of self-awareness and self-control that empowers us to respond to life's challenges with clarity and purpose. At its core, self-regulation involves managing our emotional responses in a way that aligns with our values and long-term goals. Emotions are like wild stallions, untamed and unpredictable, but with self-regulation, we can harness their power and channel it towards constructive ends. Whether it's managing feelings of anger during a heated argument or resisting the temptation to indulge in unhealthy habits, self-regulation enables us to stay true to ourselves and make decisions that serve our highest good. One of the key pillars of self-regulation is emotional control. Emotions have a way of hijacking our rational minds, leading us to act impulsively or irrationally in the heat of the moment. By developing emotional control, we can ride the waves of our emotions with grace and resilience, rather than being swept away by them. This involves cultivating mindfulness and self-awareness, tuning into our emotional experiences with curiosity and non-judgmental awareness. Through practices such as meditation, deep breathing, and mindfulness, we can develop greater emotional resilience and flexibility, enabling us to respond to life's challenges with clarity and composure. Moreover, self-regulation entails managing our impulses and urges with discipline and restraint. In today's fast-paced world, where instant gratification is just a click away, resisting temptation can be a Herculean task. However, with self-regulation, we can pause and consider the consequences of our actions before acting upon them. This involves setting clear boundaries and goals for ourselves, as well as developing strategies to overcome temptation and stay focused on what truly matters. By exercising discipline and self-control, we can avoid succumbing to the lure of immediate gratification and make decisions that align with our values and long-term aspirations. Furthermore, self-regulation involves cultivating cognitive control — the ability to regulate our thoughts and attention with focus and clarity. In today's hyper-connected world, our attention is constantly bombarded by distractions and stimuli, making it challenging to stay focused and productive. However, with self-regulation, we can filter out distractions, stay present in the moment, and direct our attention towards tasks that matter most. This involves practicing mindfulness and cognitive-behavioral techniques, as well as setting clear priorities and boundaries for ourselves. By developing cognitive control, we can enhance our productivity and performance, as well as improve our overall well-being and quality of life. Self-regulation is also essential for fostering resilience in the face of adversity. Life is full of challenges and setbacks, but with self-regulation, we can bounce back stronger and more determined than before. This involves cultivating a growth mindset — a belief that our abilities and talents can be developed through dedication and effort. By reframing challenges as opportunities for growth and learning, we can cultivate resilience and perseverance in the face of adversity. Moreover, self-regulation enables us to regulate our responses to stress and adversity, allowing us to maintain composure and make rational decisions even in the most challenging of circumstances.

5.3 Cultivating Empathy

Cultivating empathy is akin to nurturing a delicate flower in the garden of human relationships. It requires tender care, patience, and a genuine desire to understand and connect with others on a deeper emotional level. Empathy is more than just recognizing and acknowledging another person's feelings; it's about stepping into their shoes, seeing the world through their eyes, and feeling what they feel. In today's fast-paced and often disconnected world, cultivating empathy is more important than ever. It serves as the glue that binds individuals together, fostering trust, compassion, and cooperation in personal and professional relationships. At its essence, empathy is about tuning into the emotional experiences of others with an open heart and mind. It involves active listening, genuine curiosity, and a willingness to suspend judgment and truly engage with another person's perspective. When we cultivate empathy, we create a safe and supportive space where others feel seen, heard, and valued for who they are. This sense of validation and understanding forms the foundation of healthy and fulfilling relationships, enabling individuals to connect authentically and build mutual trust and respect. Moreover, empathy plays a crucial role in effective communication and conflict resolution. When we approach interactions with empathy, we demonstrate a sincere interest in understanding others' perspectives and feelings. This creates an atmosphere of openness and trust, making it easier to communicate honestly and resolve conflicts constructively. Rather than reacting defensively or dismissively to differing viewpoints, empathetic individuals strive to find common ground and work towards mutually beneficial solutions. By fostering empathy in our interactions, we can break down barriers, bridge differences, and cultivate stronger, more harmonious relationships. Furthermore, empathy is a powerful tool for supporting others during times of need or distress. When we empathize with someone who is experiencing pain or suffering, we offer them the invaluable gift of validation and emotional support. Empathy allows us to connect with others on a human level, offering a shoulder to lean on and a listening ear without judgment or criticism. Through acts of empathy and compassion, we can provide comfort, reassurance, and encouragement to those who are struggling, helping them feel less alone and more supported in their journey. Cultivating empathy also involves developing self-awareness and emotional regulation skills. By understanding our own emotions and triggers, we can better empathize with others and respond to their needs with greater sensitivity and compassion. Additionally, practicing self-care and stress management techniques can help prevent empathy fatigue and burnout, allowing us to continue supporting others effectively over the long term.

5.4 Navigating Social Skills

Navigating social skills is akin to traversing a vast and intricate web of human interactions, where every connection and encounter presents an opportunity for growth and connection. In today's interconnected world, where relationships play a crucial role in personal and professional success, mastering social skills is more important than ever. Social skills encompass a wide range of abilities, from effective communication and active listening to empathy, conflict resolution, and networking. By honing these skills, individuals can navigate social situations with confidence, build meaningful relationships, and achieve their goals. Effective communication lies at the heart of strong social skills. It involves more than just conveying information; it's about expressing oneself clearly, listening attentively, and understanding others' perspectives. Effective communicators are adept at verbal and nonverbal communication, using body language, tone of voice, and facial expressions to convey their message accurately. They also pay attention to their audience, adjusting their communication style and approach to suit the situation and the individuals involved. Active listening is another critical component of social skills. It involves fully engaging with others, demonstrating genuine interest and empathy, and seeking to understand their thoughts, feelings, and concerns. Active listeners refrain from interrupting or passing judgment, instead focusing on truly hearing and validating the speaker's perspective. By practicing active listening, individuals can foster trust, build rapport, and strengthen their relationships with others. Empathy is perhaps one of the most valuable social skills, as it allows individuals to connect with others on a deeper emotional level. Empathy involves understanding and sharing the feelings of others, acknowledging their experiences, and responding with compassion and kindness. Empathetic individuals are attuned to the emotions of those around them, offering support and encouragement when needed and celebrating others' successes and joys. By cultivating empathy, individuals can foster strong bonds and create a sense of belonging and connection in their relationships. Conflict resolution is another essential social skill that enables individuals to navigate disagreements and conflicts constructively. Effective conflict resolution involves communication, negotiation, and problem-solving skills, as well as empathy and emotional intelligence. Individuals who excel at conflict resolution can address conflicts calmly and respectfully, finding mutually acceptable solutions that satisfy the needs and interests of all parties involved. By approaching conflicts with empathy and understanding, individuals can preserve relationships and promote positive outcomes. Networking is a social skill that is particularly valuable in professional settings. It involves building and maintaining relationships with colleagues, mentors, clients, and other professionals to expand one's professional network and seize new opportunities. Effective networkers are genuine, proactive, and generous in their interactions, seeking to build authentic connections based on mutual respect and trust. By cultivating a strong professional network, individuals can access valuable resources, support, and career opportunities that can propel their professional growth and success.

5.5 Managing Motivation

Managing motivation is akin to tending to a delicate flame within oneself – it requires careful nurturing, protection from external forces, and occasional stoking to keep it burning brightly. Motivation, the driving force behind our actions and behaviors, plays a pivotal role in propelling us toward our goals and aspirations. It is what fuels our pursuit of excellence, empowers us to overcome obstacles, and sustains our efforts even in the face of adversity. At its core, effective motivation management begins with self-awareness – an understanding of one's values, desires, strengths, and weaknesses. By recognizing what truly matters to us and aligning our goals with our intrinsic motivations, we can ignite a sense of purpose and passion that propels us forward. Self-awareness allows us to set meaningful and achievable goals that resonate with our deepest aspirations, increasing our likelihood of success and fulfillment. However, managing motivation goes beyond mere self-awareness; it also entails self-regulation – the ability to control one's impulses, emotions, and behaviors in pursuit of long-term goals. Self-regulation enables individuals to stay focused and disciplined, resisting the temptation of immediate gratification in favor of long-term rewards. It involves setting clear boundaries, establishing effective routines, and managing stress effectively to maintain momentum and avoid burnout. One key aspect of managing motivation is understanding the difference between intrinsic and extrinsic motivation. While extrinsic motivators such as rewards, recognition, or praise can provide temporary boosts in motivation, true fulfillment comes from within – from aligning our actions with our values, passions, and aspirations. By cultivating intrinsic motivation – the inherent drive to pursue activities for their own sake – individuals can sustain their enthusiasm and commitment over the long term, even when external rewards are scarce. Moreover, effective motivation management involves fostering a growth mindset – the belief that our abilities and intelligence can be developed through dedication and effort. A growth mindset enables individuals to view challenges and setbacks as opportunities for learning and growth rather than insurmountable obstacles. By embracing a growth mindset, individuals can cultivate resilience and perseverance, bouncing back from failures with renewed determination and optimism. To manage motivation effectively, it is essential to create an environment that supports and nurtures it. Surrounding oneself with supportive and like-minded individuals, seeking out inspiring role models, and celebrating progress and achievements along the way can all contribute to maintaining high levels of motivation. Additionally, setting clear expectations, breaking goals down into manageable steps, and rewarding oneself for progress can help sustain motivation over the long term.

5.7 Promoting Leadership and Collaboration

Promoting leadership and collaboration is not just about achieving individual success; it's about fostering a culture of teamwork, innovation, and shared purpose that benefits everyone involved. In today's interconnected and rapidly changing world, the ability to lead effectively and collaborate with others is essential for navigating complex challenges and seizing new opportunities. Whether in the workplace, community, or any other setting, promoting leadership and collaboration can drive positive change, foster innovation, and achieve collective success. Leadership is about more than just holding a position of authority; it's about inspiring and motivating others to work towards a common vision or goal. Effective leaders lead by example, demonstrating integrity, empathy, and a commitment to excellence in all that they do. They empower others to succeed, provide guidance and support when needed, and foster a culture of trust, respect, and collaboration. By promoting leadership, individuals can inspire others to reach their full potential, drive innovation, and achieve collective goals. Collaboration, on the other hand, is about working effectively with others to achieve shared objectives. It involves communication, teamwork, and a willingness to share ideas, resources, and expertise for the greater good. Collaboration enables individuals to leverage diverse perspectives, skills, and experiences to solve complex problems, generate new ideas, and drive innovation. By promoting collaboration, individuals can break down silos, foster creativity, and achieve outcomes that exceed what any individual could accomplish alone. One of the key ingredients for promoting leadership and collaboration is cultivating empathy – the ability to understand and share the feelings of others. Empathy enables individuals to connect with others on a deeper level, build trust and rapport, and resolve conflicts constructively. By cultivating empathy, individuals can foster a culture of understanding, compassion, and inclusivity, where everyone feels valued, respected, and empowered to contribute their unique perspectives and talents. Another essential component is developing strong social skills and emotional intelligence. Social skills enable individuals to communicate effectively, build rapport, and resolve conflicts, while emotional intelligence allows individuals to recognize, understand, and manage their own emotions, as well as the emotions of others. By developing these skills, individuals can navigate complex social dynamics, build strong relationships, and lead and collaborate effectively with others. Promoting leadership and collaboration also requires creating an environment that supports and encourages these behaviors. This includes providing opportunities for leadership development and training, fostering a culture of open communication and constructive feedback, and recognizing and rewarding collaboration and teamwork. By creating an environment where leadership and collaboration are valued and encouraged, individuals can unleash the full potential of their teams and achieve remarkable results.

CHAPTER SIX

CONCLUSION: THE PATH FORWARD

As we come to the conclusion of our journey exploring emotional intelligence and its transformative power, it's essential to reflect on the key takeaways and consider the path forward for ongoing practice and growth.

Throughout this exploration, we've delved into various aspects of emotional intelligence, from self-awareness and self-regulation to empathy, social skills, and leadership. We've learned that emotional intelligence serves as a fundamental pillar for personal and professional success, enabling individuals to navigate complex social dynamics, build strong relationships, and achieve their goals with resilience and determination.

One of the central themes that emerged is the importance of self-awareness – the foundation upon which emotional intelligence is built. By understanding our thoughts, emotions, and behaviors, we can identify our strengths and weaknesses, cultivate resilience, and make informed decisions that align with our values and aspirations. Self-awareness empowers us to recognize our emotional triggers, regulate our responses, and navigate challenges with grace and confidence.

Similarly, self-regulation plays a crucial role in emotional intelligence, enabling us to manage our emotions, impulses, and behaviors effectively, even in challenging or stressful situations. By harnessing self-regulation, we can maintain composure, make rational decisions, and resist impulses that may undermine our goals or values, thus positioning ourselves for success in various aspects of life.

Empathy and social skills are also integral components of emotional intelligence, allowing us to connect with others on a deeper level, build trust and rapport, and foster collaboration and cooperation. Cultivating empathy enables us to understand and share the feelings of others, fostering compassion and understanding in our interactions. Meanwhile, honing our social skills equips us with the tools to communicate effectively, resolve conflicts constructively, and build strong, meaningful relationships.

Leadership, too, emerges as a critical aspect of emotional intelligence, as effective leaders inspire and motivate others, drive innovation, and achieve shared goals and objectives. By promoting leadership and collaboration, individuals can create a culture of teamwork, inclusivity, and mutual support, thus maximizing the potential of their teams and achieving remarkable results together.

As we reflect on these key takeaways, it's essential to recognize that emotional intelligence is not a fixed trait but rather a skill that can be developed and honed over time with practice and dedication. Encouraging ongoing practice and growth is crucial for unleashing the full potential of emotional intelligence and realizing the transformative power it holds.

Embracing a growth mindset allows us to approach challenges as opportunities for learning and growth, rather than obstacles to be overcome. By committing to continuous self-improvement and seeking feedback from others, we can deepen our understanding of ourselves and refine our emotional intelligence skills, thus positioning ourselves for greater success and fulfillment in all areas of life.

In closing, the transformative power of emotional intelligence lies in its ability to empower individuals to navigate life's challenges with resilience, empathy, and authenticity. By embracing the principles of emotional intelligence and committing to ongoing practice and growth, we can unlock our full potential, build meaningful relationships, and achieve our goals with confidence and purpose. As we continue on our journey forward, let us remember that emotional intelligence is not just a destination but a lifelong pursuit – a journey of self-discovery, growth, and transformation.

Glossary

Active Listening: The practice of fully concentrating, understanding, responding, and remembering what is being said in a conversation.

Authenticity: The quality of being genuine, true to one's own personality, values, and spirit, regardless of external pressures.

Body Language: Nonverbal communication through gestures, facial expressions, behaviors, and posture.

Collaboration: Working together with one or more people to complete a task or achieve a goal.

Communication: The imparting or exchanging of information or news.

Compassion: Sympathetic consciousness of others' distress together with a desire to alleviate it.

Compassionate Communication: Communicating in a way that is kind and understanding, showing concern for others' well-being.

Conflict Management: The practice of recognizing and dealing with disputes in a rational, balanced, and effective way.

Conflict Resolution: The process of resolving a dispute or disagreement through constructive dialogue and negotiation.

Curiosity: A strong desire to know or learn something, often leading to exploration and discovery.

Diversity: The inclusion of different types of people (such as people of different races, cultures, genders, etc.) in a group or organization.

Emotional Intelligence (EI): The ability to recognize, understand, manage, and use emotions effectively in oneself and in others.

Emotional Regulation: The ability to respond to the ongoing demands of experience with the range of emotions in a manner that is socially tolerable and sufficiently flexible to permit spontaneous reactions as well as the ability to delay spontaneous reactions as needed.

Empathetic Leadership: Leading by understanding and sharing the feelings of team members.

Empathy: The ability to understand and share the feelings of another person.

Ethics: Moral principles that govern a person's behavior or the conducting of an activity.

Feedback: Information about reactions to a product, a person's performance of a task, etc., used as a basis for improvement.

Goal Setting: The process of identifying something that you want to accomplish and establishing measurable objectives and timeframes.

Growth Mindset: The belief that abilities and intelligence can be developed with effort and perseverance.

Humility: A modest or low view of one's own importance; humbleness.

Inclusivity: The practice or policy of including people who might otherwise be excluded or marginalized.

Influence: The capacity to have an effect on the character, development, or behavior of someone or something.

Innovation: The process of translating an idea or invention into a good or service that creates value.

Intrinsic Motivation: Doing something because it is inherently interesting or enjoyable, rather than for some separable consequence.

Leadership: The action of leading a group of people or an organization, or the ability to do this.

Listening Skills: Abilities associated with understanding, interpreting, and evaluating what is heard.

Mindfulness: The quality or state of being conscious or aware of something, often through a focus on the present moment.

Networking: Interacting with others to exchange information and develop professional or social contacts.

Nonverbal Communication: Conveying information without the use of words, including gestures, body language, and facial expressions.

Open-Mindedness: The willingness to consider new ideas; unprejudiced.

Patience: The capacity to accept or tolerate delay, trouble, or suffering without getting angry or upset.

Personal Development: Activities that improve awareness and identity, develop talents and potential, enhance quality of life, and contribute to the realization of dreams and aspirations.

Perspective-Taking: The ability to understand a situation or concept from an alternative point of view.

Positive Reinforcement: The addition of a reward following a desired behavior, making it more likely to happen in the future.

Problem-Solving: The process of finding solutions to difficult or complex issues.

Rapport: A close and harmonious relationship in which the people or groups concerned understand each other's feelings or ideas and communicate well.

Resilience: The capacity to recover quickly from difficulties; toughness.

Resilient Leadership: Leading with the ability to recover quickly from setbacks and adversity, maintaining focus and determination in the face of challenges.

Self-Awareness: Conscious knowledge of one's own character, feelings, motives, and desires.

Self-Regulation: The ability to manage one's behavior, emotions, and thoughts in pursuit of long-term goals.

Social Awareness: The ability to take the perspective of and empathize with others from diverse backgrounds and cultures.

Social Skills: Skills used to communicate and interact with others effectively.

Stress Management: Techniques and therapies that help a person control their level of stress, especially chronic stress.

Support System: A network of people who provide an individual with practical or emotional support.

Teamwork: The combined action of a group of people, especially when effective and efficient.

Time Management: The ability to use one's time effectively or productively, especially at work.

Trust: Firm belief in the reliability, truth, ability, or strength of someone or something.

Values: A person's principles or standards of behavior; one's judgment of what is important in life.

Vision: The ability to think about or plan the future with imagination or wisdom.

Work-Life Balance: The equilibrium between personal life and career work.

Ahad, R., Mustafa, M. Z., Mohamad, S., Abdullah, N. H. S., & Nordin, M. N. (2021). Work attitude, organizational commitment and emotional intelligence of Malaysian vocational college teachers. *Journal of Technical Education and Training, 13*(1), 15-21.

Alonazi, W. B. (2020). The impact of emotional intelligence on job performance during COVID-19 crisis: A cross-sectional analysis. *Psychology Research and Behavior Management*, 749-757.

Alzoubi, H. M., & Aziz, R. (2021). Does emotional intelligence contribute to quality of strategic decisions? The mediating role of open innovation. *Journal of Open Innovation: Technology, Market, and Complexity, 7*(2), 130.

Boyatzis, R. E. (2018). The behavioral level of emotional intelligence and its measurement. *Frontiers in psychology, 9*, 385616.

Bradberry, T., & Greaves, J. (2006). *The emotional intelligence quick book: Everything you need to know to put your EQ to work*. Simon and Schuster.

Bradberry, T., & Greaves, J. (2009). *Emotional Intelligence 2.0*. TalentSmart.

Cejudo, J., Rodrigo-Ruiz, D., López-Delgado, M. L., & Losada, L. (2018). Emotional intelligence and its relationship with levels of social anxiety and stress in adolescents. *International journal of environmental research and public health, 15*(6), 1073.

Chen, J., & Guo, W. (2020). Emotional intelligence can make a difference: The impact of principals' emotional intelligence on teaching strategy mediated by instructional leadership. *Educational Management Administration & Leadership, 48*(1), 82-105.

Chernis, C., & Adler, M. (2023). *Promoting emotional intelligence in organizations*. Association for Talent Development.

Ciarrochi, J., Forgas, J. P., & Mayer, J. D. (Eds.). (2013). *Emotional intelligence in everyday life*. Psychology press.

Cleary, M., Visentin, D., West, S., Lopez, V., & Kornhaber, R. (2018). Promoting emotional intelligence and resilience in undergraduate nursing students: An integrative review. *Nurse education today, 68*, 112-120.

Domínguez-García, E., & Fernández-Berrocal, P. (2018). The association between emotional intelligence and suicidal behavior: A systematic review. *Frontiers in psychology, 9*, 360917.

Drigas, A. S., & Papoutsi, C. (2018). A new layered model on emotional intelligence. *Behavioral sciences, 8*(5), 45.

Drigas, A., & Papoutsi, C. (2020). The Need for Emotional Intelligence Training Education in Critical and Stressful Situations: The Case of Covid-19. *Int. J. Recent Contributions Eng. Sci. IT, 8*(3), 20-36.

Extremera Pacheco, N., Rey Peña, L., & Sánchez Álvarez, N. (2019). Validation of the Spanish version of the Wong Law emotional intelligence scale (WLEIS-S). *Psicothema*.

Extremera, N., Mérida-López, S., Sánchez-Álvarez, N., & Quintana-Orts, C. (2018). How does emotional intelligence make one feel better at work? The mediational role of work engagement. *International journal of environmental research and public health, 15*(9), 1909.

Goleman, D. (2020). *Emotional intelligence*. Bloomsbury Publishing.

Goleman, D. (2021). *Leadership: The power of emotional intelligence*. More Than Sound LLC.

Gómez-Leal, R., Holzer, A. A., Bradley, C., Fernández-Berrocal, P., & Patti, J. (2022). The relationship between emotional intelligence and leadership in school leaders: A systematic review. *Cambridge Journal of Education, 52*(1), 1-21.

Guerra-Bustamante, J., León-del-Barco, B., Yuste-Tosina, R., López-Ramos, V. M., & Mendo-Lázaro, S. (2019). Emotional intelligence and psychological well-being in adolescents. *International journal of environmental research and public health, 16*(10), 1720.

Hasan, M. M., & Chowdhury, S. A. (2023). Relationship Between Education, Emotional Intelligence, and Sustainable Behavior Change Among College Students in Bangladesh. *Education & Learning in Developing Nations, 1* (1), 1–4.

Issah, M. (2018). Change leadership: The role of emotional intelligence. *Sage Open, 8*(3), 2158244018800910.

Jordan, P. J., & Troth, A. C. (2021). Managing emotions during team problem solving: Emotional intelligence and conflict resolution. In *Emotion and Performance* (pp. 195-218). CRC Press.

Kant, R. (2019). Emotional intelligence: A study on university students. *Journal of Education and Learning (EduLearn)*, *13*(4), 441-446.

Kotsou, I., Mikolajczak, M., Heeren, A., Grégoire, J., & Leys, C. (2019). Improving emotional intelligence: A systematic review of existing work and future challenges. *Emotion Review*, *11*(2), 151-165.

Lee, C., & Wong, C. S. (2019). The effect of team emotional intelligence on team process and effectiveness. *Journal of Management & Organization*, *25*(6), 844-859.

MacCann, C., Jiang, Y., Brown, L. E., Double, K. S., Bucich, M., & Minbashian, A. (2020). Emotional intelligence predicts academic performance: A meta-analysis. *Psychological bulletin*, *146*(2), 150.

Miao, C., Humphrey, R. H., & Qian, S. (2018). Emotional intelligence and authentic leadership: A meta-analysis. *Leadership & Organization Development Journal*, *39*(5), 679-690.

O'Connor, P. J., Hill, A., Kaya, M., & Martin, B. (2019). The measurement of emotional intelligence: A critical review of the literature and recommendations for researchers and practitioners. *Frontiers in psychology*, *10*, 1116.

Papoutsi, C., Drigas, A., & Skianis, C. (2019). Emotional intelligence as an important asset for HR in organizations: Attitudes and working variables. *International Journal of Advanced Corporate Learning*, *12*(2), 21.

Pekaar, K. A., Bakker, A. B., van der Linden, D., & Born, M. P. (2018). Self-and other-focused emotional intelligence: Development and validation of the Rotterdam Emotional Intelligence Scale (REIS). *Personality and Individual Differences*, *120*, 222-233.

Petrides, K. V., Sanchez-Ruiz, M. J., Siegling, A. B., Saklofske, D. H., & Mavroveli, S. (2018). Emotional intelligence as personality: Measurement and role of trait emotional intelligence in educational contexts. *Emotional intelligence in education: Integrating research with practice*, 49-81.

Prentice, C., Dominique Lopes, S., & Wang, X. (2020). Emotional intelligence or artificial intelligence–an employee perspective. *Journal of Hospitality Marketing & Management*, *29*(4), 377-403.

Raghubir, A. E. (2018). Emotional intelligence in professional nursing practice: A concept review using Rodgers's evolutionary analysis approach. *International journal of nursing sciences*, *5*(2), 126-130.

Ryback, D. (2012). *Putting emotional intelligence to work*. Routledge.

Sharon, D., & Grinberg, K. (2018). Does the level of emotional intelligence affect the degree of success in nursing studies?. *Nurse education today*, *64*, 21-26.

Stein, S. J., & Book, H. E. (2011). *The EQ edge: Emotional intelligence and your success*. John Wiley & Sons.

Valente, S., Monteiro, A. P., & Lourenço, A. A. (2019). The relationship between teachers' emotional intelligence and classroom discipline management. *Psychology in the Schools*, *56*(5), 741-750.

Wahyudi, W. (2018). The influence of emotional intelligence, competence and work environment on teacher performance of SMP Kemala Bhayangkari Jakarta. *Scientific Journal Of Reflection: Economic, Accounting, Management and Business*, *1*(2), 211-220.

Wen, J., Huang, S. S., & Hou, P. (2019). Emotional intelligence, emotional labor, perceived organizational support, and job satisfaction: A moderated mediation model. *International Journal of Hospitality Management*, *81*, 120-130.

Wu, Y., Lian, K., Hong, P., Liu, S., Lin, R. M., & Lian, R. (2019). Teachers' emotional intelligence and self-efficacy: Mediating role of teaching performance. *Social Behavior and Personality: an international journal*, *47*(3), 1-10.